OUR LIFE EDGING UP THE SLOPE

From Bright Blue to Light Grey

Peter Riley

Sarum

Copyright © 2022 Peter Riley

Published internationally by Sarum

Hinckley UK.

©Peter Riley 2022

The right of Peter Riley to be identified as the author has been asserted in accordance with sections 77 and 78 of the
Copyright Designs and Patents Act 1988. All rights reserved.

This book is sold subject to the condition that shall not, by way of trade or otherwise, be lent, resold, hired out or circulated without the publisher's consent in any form other than this current form and without a similar condition being imposed on a subsequent purchaser.

Any similarity between the characters and situations and places or persons, living or dead, is unintentional and co-incidental.

CONTENTS

Title Page
Copyright
Abstract
Preface
LIFE   1
Chapter 1 - Beginnings   2
Chapter 2 – Growing up   10
Chapter 3 – Higher Education and Fate   29
Chapter 4 – Professional Training and First Real Job.   39
Chapter 5 – Settling down.   52
Chapter 6 – Atomic Power   58
Chapter 7 – Head Office   66
Chapter 8 – The Republic of Korea   76
Chapter 9 – Project Management   93
Chapter 10 – Sizewell 'B' Pressurised Water Reactor   103
Chapter 11 - Retirement   113
Chapter 12 – An Academic Venture   122
Chapter 13 – Shades of Blue   128
Chapter 14 – Reflections   139

ABSTRACT

AN EVENTFUL POSITIVE STORY OF A LIFETIME: Interlaced with whimsical comment, Peter in his late eighties recounts the uncertainties of the 1930s, the BLITZ, basic schooling, the benefit of advanced education at the State's expense. He recalls achieving Engineering Fellowship in industry modernizing steel production, power generation, primarily nuclear, and latterly railways in the UK, India, and The Republic of Korea. Peter tracks his re-education in later life to participate in environmental improvement in Power. He recounts his personal involvement in care and volunteering with People Affected by Dementia and fears of reversion to politics of yesteryear.

PREFACE

Until old age loomed and then isolation imposed by the COVID-19 enforced precautions in the winter of twenty, I was confident that I knew myself. The slow approach of the grand reaper triggered the need to tidy up records and to compile sketch books to help fading memories. Stacked notebooks and diaries on shelves in the garage, boxes of photographs that Myra had classified and files in the study covering education, training, and business. The task was constantly put off until the first year of the COVID lockdown. I started to systematically plough through shelves of information making brief notes to help my ageing memory. I now have no excuse to avoid any longer delaying the process of distilling this information into what I hope is a readable story supplemented by memoirs.

LIFE

Early years protected

misdemeanours undetected

mix of pleasure and pain.

Youthful life experiences and interest in sciences

future mapped out clear.

Opportunities real and new

romances deep but few.

Full life-consuming time.

Success at last with coupling

productive and uncomplaining

perfect for half a century.

Memory and functions fade, scenes no longer made.

Last breath in oblivion.

CHAPTER 1 - BEGINNINGS

The nineteen thirties, a generation born into an era of uncertainty. Recovery from the recession of the twenties was slow due to lack of investment, risktakers were not encouraged by activities of the extreme right leadership in Italy and Germany, invasion of Ethiopia and Poland, and weak leadership in the United Kingdom. Evidence flaunted of their disciplined forces by both the fascist nations and the treatment of Jewish and underprivileged peoples was threatening. News broadcasts of the late thirties reported the continuing build-up of German troops and equipment together with the suffering of peoples in Belgium and Holland. Old enough to feel the fear in parents, the hopes of my generation limited to the very-near future and threats to a way of life. That is where this story starts.

Industry was beginning to come to life after the effects of the depression and the threat of war was mobilising heavy industry. Steel plate factories were stirring to life in response to messages coming from the continent and the need for armaments. Germany had introduced compulsory military service, Mussolini invaded Ethiopia and the Nazis enacted Nuremburg laws against Jewish people. In the Midlands, emphasis was on King George V's Silver Jubilee in a vain attempt to ease the pains of unemployment and fear of war. John Riley, the eldest boy of a family of thirteen, was a plumber but with little chance of employment as housebuilding had stagnated. John called 'Jack', was qualified following an apprenticeship and educated at the Bluecoat School in Walsall, earning his place by a scholarship. He was courting Grace, youngest daughter of a family of fourteen. Grace was working as a chambermaid for a solicitor's family in the posh part of the village at the edge of Sutton Park. Grace was the youngest of a family of fourteen living in Abbots Bromley, her dad was a steeplejack and spent much of his time on the three spires of Lichfield Cathedral. Grace had obtained a scholarship to the Girls School in Abbots Bromley but could not take it up as the family could not afford the school uniforms. Later that year a hasty marriage took place, and I was born the following March at the home of Emily, the eldest daughter of the family. Two generations later revealed that Emily was Grandma's love child. She was the kindest of the aunts confirmed by sheltering my parents. Mum's ex-employer owned the semi-detached next to my grandparent's house and rented it to dad. By the start of the war our family had grown: sister Jill, with sister Pat on the way. I have scant memories of those early years other than of a holiday mum and dad took me, a two-year-old, with Aunty Doris, Uncle Bert, and daughter Shelia to Margate. Can still remember riding on Uncle's shoulders in a punt around Dreamland. Vague memories of the uncles living next door, making a trolly for me and pushing me around the garden paths. A sense of loss when called up to the armed forces. Uncle Joe, the only one married, was a carpenter and a provider of hand-made toys when he visited.

One distinct memory was of Grandad's roses in his front garden. These were considered the healthiest in the neighbourhood. The secret lay in the feed: three houses down the hill was a small dairy, and early in the mornings the milkman would leave his pony straining to pull the trap with fresh milk in stainless steel churns up the hill past our houses. Grandad would be standing in wait with bucket and shovel and as the pony relieved itself, would dart behind the trap to scoop up the deposit before oncoming traffic. After time to mature, the roses would benefit.

I was three years old when the United Kingdom joined France and declared war on Germany in September 1939 and with immanent risk of invasion the country's workforce was mobilised. Fathers, older children, and uncles separated from families. The anticipation of a German invasion was near when air-raids began. Dad had found employment at a local factory converted to the manufacture of Bakelite cases for hand grenades, a brittle plastic, previously used for unbreakable crockery. An essential worker supporting the factory services, Dad was exempt from military duties but joined the Home Guard.

Daytime was interspersed with domestic matters. Monday: the washing with Mum and Granny, pounding the wash in a coal fired heated tub in the wash house. Squeezing washed clothes through the wringer being careful not to pinch their fingers between the rollers before stringing it out to dry along the clothesline down the garden. Every activity interrupted by listening carefully on the battery-powered wireless to the news bulletins on progress of the war, and warnings about taking care with blackout measures.

Daily life took on a more disciplined aspect. For elder males, training for duties in the home guard, air raid wardens and ambulance drivers, and for single women jobs in munitions factories and the Land-army. Mothers now the only adults present in families, with husbands in the forces or in essential occupations working long hours. Rationing of all the regular needs was in place, careful budgeting was necessary from the daily bread and milk to shoes and clothing. Children took on daily tasks to ease Mother's load. Entertainment was the radio, workers playtime at mid-day and Vera Lynn with messages of hope.

The first action to move into Europe was halted by the German army leading to a massive evacuation of British troops from Dunkirk. While it did little to the national confidence, the public showed a common resolve by the action of seagoing folk in helping to support the navy in the operation to return the troops. War was brought nearer to home with the start of massive air-raids by German bombers on industrial and commercial centres. In the midlands, the munition factories in towns surrounding Birmingham were being bombed on a nightly basis. The village was north of Birmingham with open country between, and the factories close meant that nightly we would on the sound of a siren leave our beds for the air-raid shelter. Nights spent watching the searchlights, listening to anti-aircraft fire, and the drone of enemy bombers overhead. A direct hit on the Kynocks factory, only four miles away had been effective, due to a roof light left open lighting the factory roof to make a target. It was rumoured to have been deliberate action by a fifth columnist.

One uncle was in Sri Lanka, one in the desert, one in the marines and one waiting to go back to France. The aunts, one recently bereaved with an eight-year-old daughter and one an ambulance driver, were on hand to help mum with me, a four-year-old boy, and a one-year-old girl, Jill.

The night was full of apprehension and fear waiting for the siren warning to take shelter as the German bombers were on their way to release the bombloads on the factories of Birmingham and Coventry and then turning to return, releasing any leftovers on outlying villages. Rarely a night went by without being roused from bed, down the stairs and out to the Anderson shelter in the garden, a corrugated iron tunnel like shell sunk partly in the ground and covered with turf. The tricky bits were negotiating the stairs in the dark, with my baby sister just able to walk and my aunt or her daughter Shelia helping mum, pregnant with Pat. Then down into the shelter with dim torches onto benches of wood on bricks. The skies crisscrossed with searchlight beams from the nearby Anti-Aircraft unit, the rumble of gunfire, the thump-thump-thump of the Messerschmidt engines and the deafening crash as a wayward bomb landed nearby. Playing games by torchlight until the all-clear siren, the welcome fresh air after the dank shelter atmosphere, crossing to the back door seeing a sky peppered with smoke bursts from shells and the rosy, red reflection on clouds from burning fires – a daily routine. Richard, born in

1943, increased our little group in the shelter.

It seemed endless: night after night similar, daytime fearfully listening to the news, the coming night worrying about talk of our soldiers going back to France and the possibility of being driven back again. Seeing the reality of this punishing period was the incentive that brought the USA into the war and to provide support with food supplies, allowing a build-up of defences and preparation for the eventual invasion of Normandy on D-day.

The uncles and men in the neighbourhood had left to join-up in the forces. As far as I was concerned, the ladies were in charge, and all were old. The dominant figure in my memory was Grannie, living next door, a large buxom figure who took no nonsense and always had a remedy: Epsom Salts, Cod Liver Oil, Syrup of Figs, wrap up warm and a suffocating cuddle. Grannie was superstitious and it showed in many ways: "you must never look at the new moon through the window or a mirror but if you do you must go to the bottom of the garden turn round three times saying, God bless the new moon." Aunty Doris was a widow. Her husband Bert, a carpenter, was killed when he fell from scaffolding on a school building and was pierced by the steel railings. Doris and her daughter lived with Grannie and Grandad, and also kept house for a local dentist. Auntie Doris was a source of income for me when she moved in with the dentist. She welcomed contact with the family and rewarded me for company, family gossip and to carryout errands on a Saturday morning.

Nancy, an unmarried daughter, was an ambulance driver employed with the Metropolitan, a railway carriage manufacturer in Castle Bromwich, where she waited on the senior managers in the canteen. She was a source of cigarettes, that I received help from when I was a bit older. She had a right to the goody's leftover from the dinner tables, cigarettes and chocolates. Nancy had a large boyfriend, George, who was from a couple of social classes above us and who had Sunday supper next door at Grannies, sitting on the settee and saying little. He lodged with Auntie Cath who was married to Uncle Cyril in the air force and stationed in Canada. Mum, Dad and I stayed with them for a brief period when looking for more permanent housing. Before the war Cyril was employed with the Rover as a buyer. We never found out what he did in Canada other than obtaining parts for vehicle maintenance.

Auntie Win lived in a small tenement house across the road with two young girls. Uncle Ted was in France, before the war he had been a car mechanic. When he returned after the war, he regaled us with accounts of the poverty of the people living in the devastated European industrial towns. People wheeling barrows of deutschmarks to buy bread and eating cats. One of Auntie Win's girls had rickets and was prescribed dried bananas that were collected from the food office, bananas being the last type of cargo being shipped. At Christmas and other holidays, we would come together for supper in the front room at Grannie's, Auntie Nance playing the piano and singing songs about how everything would be all right one day. The drone of the bombers, the shriek of the whistle bombs, the ack-ack fire from the batteries in Sutton Park and the crash and shock of the exploding bombs was hardly entertainment. Heavily censored airmail letters would arrive from the husbands and sons from Germany, Canada, the Middle East and somewhere in Asia. Those four or five years were a special time, Mothers had help with the children, family was sacred and the effect on me was lasting.

Grandad was ever present; his approach was alerted by the small of strong tobacco. Twist carefully prepared and loaded intone of his many pipes. He would leave his shed, a sanctuary and workplace, for a break to load and light the pipe to observe the activities around. Perhaps have a few words of wisdom or just sit on that shaded bench. He was a man of few words, not open to tell about himself. A master joiner, made cabinets, trunks, window frames and was in the process of setting up a builder's business with the son's taking up various roles. Joe and Reg carpenters, Frank a bricklayer, Bob plaster and decorator and Dad a plumber. Joe the eldest was married and lived in a house the family had built. The threat of war had brought further activity to a halt. All I know about his life outside the family is that he worked on the Canadian Pacific Railway building wooden bridges and stations. Many of the workers joined the goldrush but Grandad chose to return and worked his passage on a cattle ship to Southampton. His job was to repair the pens to confine the cattle. On arriving in England, he made his way to Tamworth and raised the family. Reports of progress dominated broadcasts as fighting was approaching Berlin. The allied front to the west under General Eisenhower and to the east under Marshal Zhukov. War ground on with Russian pressure from the east and the steady progress towards Berlin resulting in victory and celebrations. Germany surrendered unconditionally to the Russians, followed later by Japan to the USA after the explosion of two atom bombs and the awful devastation, leaving a sense of relief that was yet to take time to materialise. Things took time to ease the pressure on daily living. The immediate celebrations of VE Day, VJ Day, and the unblinding of house windows. The rationing of food, coal, clothing, and petrol continued and only gradually relaxed over the next nine years.

While reviewing this I listen to the news broadcasts of war in Ukraine with concern and anxiety just like that I experienced in the early 1940s. Although we were not displaced from our home that possibility was threatened by bomb damage or invasion of Hitler's stormtroopers. We are seeing people living in railway stations, crowding on to trains being evacuated from the cities to villages. And the relentless pressure from Russian troops.

As the workforce increased, so did the identification of unfairness in the employment system. The most independent of the workforces, melded by four years of service and experience, were less prepared for pre-war employment attitudes, conditions giving labour unions more strength to bargain, leading to disputes hindering the return to normality but making life for the working class fairer. The world was not that expected peaceful scene: the aborted Suez crisis; encirclement of Berlin and its division into eastern and western blocks; the explosion by Russia of an atom bomb; the Korean war and the explosion of a hydrogen bomb by the Americans. The tension and fear of war overhung a slow progress to stability.

CHAPTER 2 – GROWING UP

There is little record of the early days at school and early days prior to diaries and notebooks from the nineteen fifties. Significant memories of the time are vivid for selected periods and influenced my life.

On the first day at school, children were taken by the senior children as there was a general trust in local families – parents were either minding the younger children or working. That first day at school with Dad at the school room door with my forgotten gasmask is clear in my memory, as is the embarrassment of eighty-one years ago. As well as being introduced to the three Rs we were taught the regular practice of evacuation in case of air raids. With gas masks we all trooped in an orderly manner into the long tunnel, the air-raid shelter in the hill behind the school, where lessons continued.

Progress through the council school moved me from Ms. Arthur's class to Ms. Ralph's. A large red-faced voluble lady who took no prisoners, she either liked you or you were not worth the effort. She did not like dad when he was young, so I was off to a bad start. A change from Ms. Arthur who was a gentle lady but who did not spare Teddy Tingle: a ruler on the back of your hands if she judged you to be naughty.

I have little memory of this time except that I was off school for two to three weeks in the winter after changing class. I had developed headaches with visual disturbances and numbness in my left hand and cheek. I was confined to the double bed in the front bedroom heated by a gas fire. Jill and Pat were moved to share my small bedroom at the back. The headaches came in mid-morning after my vision was distorted – that I described as little men dancing on the bedrail – lasting for about an hour, followed by tingling fingers and face. Mum called the Doctor who said I had a neuralgic condition that he later described as Migraine. After a week or so the sensation stopped, and I felt normal.

Ms. Ralph's boisterous and uncaring attitude was brought home to me when I returned from a month's absence. She demanded an explanation in front of the class. Replied that I had been poorly with a mental condition. She bawled out so that all could hear "Mental condition, what do you know about that?" I was at a loss for words. Ms. Ralph taught by rote with little explanation, multiplication tables and spelling tests, us children writing using a blackboard and chalk to practice longhand. The classroom was separated from the senior class ruled by a headmaster with a rod of iron. We could hear his ranting through the glass screen separating the room. During the two years in that class, we received fearful information from overhearing the delivery of lessons from two heads: Mr. Fuster, an eccentric, carried a cane that he rapped on desks and hands. Monday Mornings we trooped to Mr. Fuster's classroom to pay milk money for the daily small bottle handed out at morning break. One day while we were queuing at the door, a policeman brought in a handcuffed eleven-year-old caught out of school, a truant. He was held over a desk by the policeman while Mr. Fuster delivered punishment by cane, saw by the queue of infants. He was later replaced by Mr. Sheppard as headmaster, equally bullying and shouting. Listening to his shouting and fearing moving to his class contributed to my development of migraine. Mum believed so and complained to the council. That did not improve Ms. Ralph's opinion of me. Moving to the senior class was not so terrifying, Mr. Green had replaced Mr. Sheppard, a recently demobbed flight crew. A more caring younger man who encouraged me to develop my artistic talent in painting, and two of my watercolours were displayed in the National Gallery's children exhibition. He persuaded me to help him paint the walls of the infant class with scenes of farming activities.

The forerunner of the Archers in stills.

The school had a playground for girls and junior boys, and another for the boys of the senior class where bullying was rife. Games were rough and tumble, typically British Bulldog that was a cruder version of the Eton Wall Game. The playground sloped and in winter slides were developed on frosty mornings, an excuse to get to school early to play before the bell to line up to go to classes. At the end of the playground was an air raid shelter that until victory in Europe we took part in regular practice led by the headmaster, an opportunity for the bully to show his control. To be caught in the tunnel at other times was an excuse for application of the cane. Outside school I had small a group of friends who lived nearby. Ray the policeman's son and I played from the age of two. We played outside in the gardens, taking our dog for a walk when older and with other boys in the woods at school age. Later we would go to the cinema in Walsall, travelling on the bus.

I kept in touch with him until weeks ago when he died with a lung condition brought on by the COVID virus.

Carl J – who came to the village as a refugee from Birmingham – was a newcomer to the village, and his dad was a manager in one of the factories. We were free to roam during daylight and when not in school we were playing with Ray and the schoolmates in the nearby fields and woods. Sunday school gave parents quiet time. I joined the Wolf Cubs and became a Sixer. My two sisters Jill and Pat started at the council school while I was there. Brother Richard was born just before the end of the war. Carole was born in 1948 on Christmas day.

Dad had been a keen football player at centre forward and he supported Aston Villa. After the war he used to take me to watch them play on Saturdays. Sitting on the top deck of a Midland Red bus he would swap experiences with the other supporters. One particularly talkative character dad referred to as "Know-all" when out of earshot. I remember the last time he took me to see the Villa play. After the match we returned, Dad to the Pub, and me home. Mum asked me what "Know-all" said, I replied that they were talking about "The Missus". Dad spent much of the time working overtime and playing Cribbage with his mates at the Hardwick Arms. Mum accepted spending the evenings alone, being able to get on with the ironing, mending, and sewing. She listened avidly to radio plays. I particularly remember the detective series, Paul Temple. Dad would get her views of his behaviour on return from the pub. On this occasion he got the full force of her tongue lashing, "You called me the Missus!!!##***." I was excluded from the football trips after that.

Gardening was delegated to me when I was strong enough to wield a spade and fork. We had chickens in a pen at the bottom of the garden that was my job to feed and keep tidy. By giving up our egg ration coupons in place of chicken feed, mostly grit, we had fresh eggs for breakfast.

Walking with a group over fields of golden stubble recently I was reminded of this time, seventy-six or more years ago.

Home from school, a quick teatime of jam sandwich and home baked cake then out to play. Crossing the newly harvested corn field to join the lads having a stubble fight. Grabbing a clump of stubble and tearing it from the earth and then winging it into the sky hoping to hit someone returning a similar missile. Our imaginary battle scene imitating hand grenades. In our minds we were on the front line.

Back from writing to reality, continuing our walk we were making our way across a vast field being harvested. Three machines were visible, one cutting the corn, the machines at least three times as large as the threshing machines of long ago, one collecting the grain that has been separated from the husks leaving a trail of headless straw that the third machine was compressing into bales. Apart from the machine drivers who were studying their iPhone there were only two humans in sight. Crossing the remaining stubble my mind drifted back to the nineteen forties.

In our street lived two farming families and at school were the children of farming families. In the summer holidays we were encouraged to go and help in the fields. The small tractor powering a harvester would be cutting and bundling the corn into sheaves tied with string and thrown to us lads, lassies, and housewives to stack into stooks. Soon the field was clear but with neat lines of the tentlike stooks left to dry for a week or so. When the farmer's field was clear the team would move on to another field.

Dried, the sheaves would be pitched onto a trailer, sometimes horse drawn, and to the farmyard to a threshing machine, belt driven through a flywheel driven by a tractor. The sheaves were then pitched by us helpers into the machine where they were deprived of the grain and ejected to be stacked. The only tool used was a pitchfork, usually seen in caricatures of the devil, but lethal if you met it. The person receiving pitched sheaves to build the stack of straw was a farm worker. We helpers were not allowed on the receiving end. Even then an essence of health and safety awareness existed. When all was gathered in, we would join in celebrating the harvest, entertained by the farmer and often with a "knees up."

In those far off days of the 1940s we could grow up, to a certain extent, in our own way. Parents had much to worry about with the threats from war and scarcity and dads and uncles far away, who knows where. We could play with our mates, the only condition being we were to be home before the allotted bedtime.

The local bobby had an autonomy in the control of children. A word of caution directly to the child and if necessary, the parent informed. The schoolteacher ruled with a rod of iron: corporal punishment allowed if caught in breach of rules, for the older boys six of the best applied with a cane to the outstretched hand. "Hold your hand out naughty boy" but not so tuneful or benevolent. This triumvirate of control: parent, police officer and schoolteacher enabled reasonable control of the primary school age child.

Our small informal gang of under eleven-year-olds populated the local countryside in the evenings, weekends, and school holidays. We built tree houses, exploited foxholes, and played elaborate games usually involving warfare or cowboys and Indians, exploring fresh territory, and making campfires. A railway line ran through our territory separated by a short wooden fence and offered a rich source of coal from the overfull coal tenders, to keep our fire burning.

It was autumn, the leaves were falling, and the grass was tinder dry following a hot, dry summer. We were careful to site our campfire in a clear space beneath a small wood of tall oak trees, mindful of the possibility of fire spreading. We had not taken account of the unthinking Ginge, who had decided the fire needed stoking with an armful of dry grass and leaves. He threw the bundle on the fire at the same instant that a strong gust of wind blew in the direction of a nearby copse. The grass caught fire and the uplift of balmy air together with an extra strong gust of wind carried a ball of flaming grass into the long dry grass at the edge of the wooded copse. We grabbed sticks and started to beat the flaming grass, but it spread faster than we could extinguish and into the trees. We followed the flames into the wood and started to circle the flaming grass; a group of teenagers hiking nearby came to our aid and a nearby farmer started to direct our efforts. The copse was bounded on three sides by open fields and our efforts to keep control of the grass fire limited the burning to ground level. The wind directed the flames towards the open fields, harvested and cleared of the sheaves of wheat and the flames extinguished by our beating at the edge of the field.

The farmer thanked us all for our efforts, he thought it was sparks from the steam train that had started the fire and we did not misinform him. Our campfire extinguished and covered with dirt we went home a little late. On return home my lateness together with my grimy hands and face did not supply a satisfactory excuse and resulted in a week confinement to home and preparation for school.

Seeds of a new future were being laid during the war, an example being the Butler Education Act that could be activated at the end of the war with raising of the school leaving age and ceasing of school fees for secondary education. Political change led to free access by examination to grammar schools, a free health service, growing access to food and clothing, increasing investment in infrastructure, house building and hope for the future. Access was now possible for working class pupils to grammar schools restricted only by the need to pass an exam, the eleven plus. The schools were subject to a national standard that meant more fairness that gave access to university education. Eased by local authority scholarships that paid fees and gave living allowances to pay for accommodation away from home. Industry and agriculture were struggling due to the lack of workforce that was still in uniform and spread throughout the world. Husbands and uncles were slowly being released from faraway places, Europe, the middle east, India, the far east, and the Americas. The shortage of workforce relaxed as the pressure to rebuild housing and industries brought pressure to demobilise.

Typically, sixty scholars joined the King Edward V1 school in Lichfield, from working class families, which was a shock to the system. The secondary modern schools were deprived of the brighter students and the existing grammar schools were having to cope with a different workload of mostly un-primed students having not been to preparatory schools. Existing students were distainful of the presence of the poorly dressed newcomers. Teachers were missing the pupils from the preparatory school they had been expecting. As the years brought uniformity, teaching adjusted, pupils reaped the benefits and altered attitudes. School holidays were an opportunity to take part-time work on the land and in construction, the health and safety rules not being an obstacle. Family holidays at the seaside became possible as travel became easier. Youth Hostelling allowed independent travel, providing you were prepared to do the chores of the hostels. t the Council school we were taught how to manage intelligence tests. That was right up my street although I struggled with the English language tests. I pulled through the tests and secured my move to the King Edward VI School in Lichfield. That summer holiday after leaving the Council school sped by, and in no time, I was being kitted out by Mum with long grey trousers, a blazer, and a cap ready for the train ride into Lichfield.

Walking yesterday we passed over the footbridge at Shakerstone, a steam locomotive was preparing to start to pull the coaches to Market Bosworth. Smoke enveloped the platform as the machine puff, puff, puffed its straining way. Reminded of that grimy scene that we lived with and the first day at King Edwards School.

Off to the railway station at Four Oaks by Midland Red bus. Uniform, cap, school tie and clean white collar. The collar was detachable as the smoky railway atmosphere blackened it during the day. Mum was saved from washing a shirt a day – just the collar. The third-class carriages crammed with blazered boys.

The introduction to King Edward's, an all-boys school was like a new world. Until 1946 it was a private fee-paying school with a history going back to the time of Samuel Johnson. Teachers were elderly and were not shy to show resentment at the influx of a clear majority of boys from working class families, particularly as they were not prepared by private tuition for the school. Fortunately, there were a proportion of teachers newly released from the armed forces accustomed to mixing with all classes of people. That gave the school a strong leadership in sport; for example, our history teacher was an international cross-country runner. We settled in, free milk at break and free dinners. Through the five years to leaving examinations (GCEs) we working-class students slowly populated the school. During the early days we adopted the nicknames that others bestowed on us.

The first year passed in an instant, ending in an examination that decided our streaming for successive years. To my surprise I was considered academic and continued to learn Latin, as opposed to the B class that dropped Latin and continued with art and woodwork. By choice I would have preferred to continue with art.

Probably this was a deciding factor for my life.

The following years I kept a position about halfway down the class list, a little higher in Mathematics and physics, and lower in English and the humanities. I enjoyed playing rugger at school, earned a position in the Colts team as hooker and by the fifth form I was a regular player for the school first team. School and home life merged, my friend Ray had gone to the Queen Mary School in Walsall, so we exchanged experiences and friends. I earned a nickname: this previously private school had an unwritten tradition. After resisting I gave in to being called 'Paddy Riley', after a character in the film, *Blue Lagoon*.

I joined the youth club and the Church Fellowship where we mixed with friends from the Council school days, older boys and girls. The club met on Friday evenings. Table tennis for a start, then a talk from the leader and a visitor, capped off with a dance, usually with gramophone records of the big bands and occasionally a live jazz band led by one of the club members playing the trumpet. Sometimes a visiting pianist would join in making the event quite professional. We put on a pantomime each year and I took on various roles. One year, Buttons in Cinderella, another a Pirate in Robinson Crusoe.

I obtained a reasonable set of passes in the General Certificate Examination to enter the Sixth Form. I prepared to leave and take an apprenticeship, but the headmaster persuaded Dad to allow me to stay on. Mum was not too happy, with me staying at school for another two years, to budget for the family of five children. I enjoyed playing rugby for a successful first team that earned me a credit and offset the failure to pass English Language in the GCE. Friends made in the sixth form and rugby teammates stayed in touch. Ron, 'Fatty', went to Canada as a geologist, then studied law and became head of the Construction Bar in Canada. He died of throat cancer in 1979. Brian, 'Tosser', graduated in medicine, became a gynaecologist, emigrated to Canada, and is now retired. 'Shrig' committed suicide while at university. 'Big Jim' became an aeronautical engineer and managing director leaving this life recently.

Dad's family were craftsmen who worked in the building trade, the most adventurous being my grandfather who before settling down helped to build the Canadian Pacific Railway. The books serialised in magazines were influential: Neville Shute's The Lonely Road and On the Beach; Hammond Innes's Campbell's Kingdom; and John Master's Bhowani Junction and Far, Far the Mountain Peak. Dad advised me to study Electrical Engineering as he, a plumber, could see the work on buildings moving to electrical lighting and cooking, away from gas and coal. Unconsciously, engineering, travel and large projects were framing my ideas for the future.

My future was being moulded.

In the science sixth form, I finally passed the English Language GCE after four attempts. Out of school Mr. Brockwell, our rugby teacher, persuaded me to play for the Lichfield City team when there was not a school game. This introduced me to the harder game, and I continued to play for Lichfield until work took me away from the area. It also helped me to get selected for the College team. Cricket was not my game: at school, on the rare occasion when I played in the inter-house tournament, I was always the last man in and often bowled out with the first ball. I just could not see it, probably because I closed my eyes in terror as the bowler thundered towards me. I was posted to the boundary when fielding and often did not prevent a four, because I closed my eyes when the ball tumbled from the sky like a comet, or because I was either daydreaming or eyeing the gym slips on the boundary. Ray, my best mate, was a good cricketer, and he lived the game. He left school after 'O' levels and had an apprenticeship with IMI in metallurgy with pay, so he could afford to join the local cricket and tennis club. On Saturday afternoons in the summer, I would go to support him but spend the time watching the girls play tennis. Après cricket started in the club house and us hangers-on were grudgingly allowed into the bar along with the tennis girls to mix with the players. Ray, my mate, was one of the younger ones and Thurston the fast bowler usually joined us. Thurston, a tall blond haired ex-scholarship boy at the school a long way ahead of us, had been disowned by his family because of an association with the opening bat. John was a middle-aged bachelor who lived with his sister. John persuaded Thurston that instead of going to university he should join him in starting up a market garden and study part-time in horticulture at the local tech. The family viewed this as a waste of a clever mind and were suspicious of John's motives, thus disowning Thurston.

The work in the market garden was piling up, partly due to the charisma of Thurston, their deputy manager, who persuaded John that he needed part-time help with the potting, tomato watering and green vegetable harvesting. I got a Saturday job that extended into the weekdays during school holidays for a shilling an hour. Thurston was an organist at a local Church and took the choir practice on Friday evenings. He sometimes made a case to John to use the Morris Twelve to go to the Church to practice on a Friday evening. When this arrangement became routine, he suggested we meet him after choir practice for a run in the countryside. Ray, Carl, and I did so, and after the expeditions became more adventurous with our having a go at driving the car and spending time at a local village pub. John lived quite close to the church, but Thurston parked out of sight. All went well till the start of the summer when I was expecting to work at the nursery to save for a youth hostelling cycle holiday. I turned up on the Saturday morning to find Thurston noticeably quiet and choosing to work at the far end of the garden. John was gruffer than usual, sending me to the greenhouse to water the tomatoes which was always unpleasant and boring but even more so on that sweltering day. Lunch time arrived and going to collect my wages I found Ray and Carl waiting outside the office looking very subdued. John came from the office with my pay packet and asked me if I had an enjoyable time on Friday night. Said that I did and that it had been a walk in Sutton Park near the church. He looked at the other two who said we all went to Blackroot pool to row. "Well, I saw you getting into my car and riding off with Thurston" he said, thrust the pay packet in my hand and said he did not want to see any of us there again, turned his back and went into the office. When I explained why I was not working on the Monday my dad said, "honesty pays, you better get off to the Labour Exchange and sign on." I did and got a job the same day on a building site at the going rate of four shillings and seven pence an hour with double time at weekend – more than four times John had paid. Cricketing afternoons had stopped, allowed me a whole day's work at double time at weekends for six weeks, so after paying Mum for my keep I was well in hand for the cycling holiday.

School was not all work and my deficient performance in English did not prevent me from reading non-approved material. In those days of innocence, other than the Beano the most sought after was a small red book, *The Red Light*. Sought after because of undeclared reasons, it was part of our education; but if a boy was discovered with it under the desk, it was confiscated and said to be destroyed by the teacher to the amusement of the older boys. Somehow the book was in a similar category to the unexpurgated version of D H Lawrence's *Lady Chatterley's Lover* that was also sought after, but riskier to have, as it meant a visit to the Headmaster's Study and six of the best unless you told him where it came from. After the famous obscenity trial of 1960, you could buy it from Smith's but by then we were better informed.

I was gradually introduced to life by experience and the tales of the older boys. It was a boys' school, accuracy of the tales that unfolded were slanted. Sixth form boys on the bus bragging about their adventures all trying to outdo the last related experience. On the train homeward being trapped in a railway carriage with a robust youth who wanted stimulation and prepared to get it by force. Pushed into a corner with his hand down my trousers while his mild companion pretending to read a history book was getting his thrill peeping over his spectacles. Parental concerns about certain middle-aged single blokes in the village, the vicar, the youth club leader, the scout leader and even the older girls at the youth club, all intended to make one aware without knowing what to expect. One heard the tales of the sixteen-year-olds that had started work in the factories that had been converted from making munitions to Bakelite tableware and other mass-produced domestic appliances. The presses that converted the powders to solid shapes were staffed by females eagerly awaiting the return of the menfolk from the forces. An initiation ceremony would be for the youth to be sent from the drawing office to deliver a vital part for a broken press to the foreman's office at the far end of the press shop, through back-to-back lines of machine operators all with waggling buttocks and exploring fingers that found their goal without the machine losing their attention. By the time, the book was available it no longer had any mystery left for the lads having received help from others' experience, imagination, outright false but exciting stories, and barber shop banter.

Reality began to dawn with the daily morning vision of that twenty-year-old smartly dressed and made-up girl at the railway station, looking like Liz Taylor and who always gave me a smile, the experience lasting till morning milk break and reducing my exam chances by attention on elsewhere than the subjects in class. The first tangible approach to female contact was on the dance floor for the last half-hour at the Friday night youth club and the ladies excuse-me quickstep when that exciting sixteen-year-old looked me in the eyes and sang, "Hey there you with your nose in the air, love never made a fool of you." Carpe Diem! But she did two years later, back to loneliness. Entranced by Jackie and gradually, as the song says, "Saw her again and again." We became a couple; she even came to watch me playing rugby. I introduced Jackie to the family one winter Sunday after skating on Bracebridge Pond in Sutton Park. Family tea when we all got together to be prepared to explain our week's activities. Jill had already introduced her first boyfriend Graham, so although nervous I took the plunge. Sitting round the table with the full family we were subject to a barrage of questions. I started to have visual disturbances that took me back to my experience as a six-year-old. The migraine had returned.

Since then, I have experienced Migraines at isolated times, rarely over extended periods but then as a cluster over days until recent years. The Medical Profession have no cure but have developed a medicine that alleviates the pain. Prior to that it was seen as psychosomatic. In 1960 the book Migraine by Oliver Sachs describes the developed knowledge of the disease in detail over the millennia. He describes the visions of Hildegard of Bingen, a nun and mystic of exceptional and literary powers, as the aura of migraine, visual disturbances, like my describing them as little men jumping on the bottom of my bed. Not a bad parallel for a six-year-old!

I have little memory of how the teatime went. It must have been successful as it was the first of many.

Back to school, we were not always following the rules even though, as prefects, we were expected to enforce them. Lunchbreak at school and a group of the upper six not on dinner duty escaped to a small transport café on the edge of town. Siting round a small table in a far corner were a group of four from the science sixth: Fatty, Tosser, Shrig and Paddy. We were from the second batch of eleven plus scholars now in their final year at Grammar School. Two were smoking and all had coffee. The conversation was initially about the weekend, interrupted by Shrig: he had heard that Big Jim, one of the group, had been bragging. He claimed he had received valentine cards from five of the girls on the school bus. "We'll have to bring him down a peg," said Fatty. Immediately Shrig had a plan and produced a copy of *Women's Own* Magazine. He suggested, "Let's fill in this application for confidential information about young pregnancies using his name, J Smith, and his address." All nodded their approval, put out the fags and left back to school. At the end of the week all four were present in the café as well as Jim. As usual fags and coffee were the priority. Hardly restraining himself Jim pulled out an envelope marked confidential addressed to Ms. J Smith and showed its contents to the lads. It was an invitation to request a confidential discussion with a nurse to discuss Ms. Smith's problem. Shrig took the letter and studied it intently, passed it round the table and then slipped it together with the stamped and addressed envelope in his bag. Shortly after it was fags out and back to school. Shrig said he had an appointment at the clinic in town and left.

In the school library two weeks later, the class were revising for a chemistry mock exam. Jim stood up and in a slightly nervous manner, which was unusual for him, announced: "Last Saturday my mother had a visit from the district nurse who wanted to see her daughter. Mum explained she did not have a daughter and was then shown an application form completed in neat capitals from Ms. Jenny Smith. Mum got a bit angry and said she would sort it out. She is going to see the Head." The class got on with the revision slightly unnerved until lunch break. Three of the usual four headed off downtown to the café and were seated there when the new art teacher, who joined the school staff after Christmas, being demobbed from the air force, came in and said approvingly, "Nice set up you have here, I didn't see cigarettes did I Paddy?" and then turned and left. The group were not long after following him.

Just before the bell went for going home the Head entered the library and said, pointing to Fatty, Tosser, Shrig and me, I want you four to come down to my room. Three entered the head's study, Shrig had left saying he had an appointment at the clinic. The Head quickly got to the point: "I have had a visit from Mrs. Smith who explained that the new health service had been put to expense and that she had been embarrassed by a practical joke that had been clearly hatched by someone in the school. Ms. Jones also visited me, Shrigley's foster mother, who explained how her charge had conditions that excused him from being here this afternoon." The Head then walked to the corner cupboard where he stored the canes and took time to select three. "I have been watching you four and once you are outside the school boundary, I cannot control what you do. Understand that Shrigley has a problem and I suspect you know that. But I do not expect you to take advantage of one of his weaknesses. You are all good scholars and fine prefects and have helped the school teams to achieve a good standing in the county. But I will not have the school associated with this behaviour." Having said that he selected one of the canes, cleared papers from a section of his oak desk, told Fatty to bend over the desk, swished the cane and then delivered six of the best across the seat of Fatty's ample posterior, Tosser and I followed. Standing there holding back our tears he informed us we were banned from leaving during school time until going home time for the rest of the term. Failure to obey would result in further punishment and loss of our prefect's role. Not the best way to end term. The other three all left for university, and I had to remain for a further year. We did enjoy a successful cycling holiday: a seventeen day eight-hundred-mile tour of the south of England, staying in youth hostels from home to Dover, along the south coast to Tavistock, back along the north coast of Cornwall, Devon, and home.

Failure to achieve a satisfactory set of A-level exam results meant that my place at Birmingham University could not be taken, but I was encouraged by the Head to try again and continue into my third year in the sixth form. Dad was all for it, but Mum with the job of bringing up a family of five would have appreciated an extra earner in the family. I secured a temporary job as a labourer on a building site that helped with the income for the summer and went back to school with a younger but even brighter science sixth form. More responsibilities as rugby vice-captain and Ashmole House Captain. When available I played with the Lichfield rugby club sometimes in the first team.

A memory I cannot forget this is a fiction describing what happened in a real match.

Musings drew back to schooldays: he Will, Big Jim and Trevor played in the first XV from the fifth form; Trevor an England Schoolboys winger; Will and Jim second row, being the tallest in the school, and Paddy as hooker. They played together for three seasons and with the local town team, seeing themselves as tops.

In that final year of A-levels all became a bit needle. In the inter-house rugby cup Will and Trevor played for Baxter House, with Paddy as the captain of Ashmole. The teams were to meet in the final. It was a typical wet, muddy winter day. Halfway through the second half with no score Darwin close to the Baxter try-line when they conceded a line-out. Will was the school line-out man and, with Baxter throw-in, was expected to catch the ball and ease the pressure on his team. This was a move that the school team had practiced to perfection. Now the two best school jumpers, Will and Big Jim, were on opposing sides. Paddy knew the routine, he moved from his usual position at the front of the line-out to be just in front of Will's position. Trevor at wing threw the ball aiming at Will's likely catching position. The ball curved high above the line-out and fell precisely towards Will's right. As he launched himself into the air and grasped the ball with his fingertips, Big Jim opposite him jumped at the same instant, stretching towards Will's shoulders. Paddy grabbed Wills ankles letting go as Will toppled with Jim on top of him.

The last time Paddy saw Will was as he lay lifeless on the stretcher to the ambulance, his face drooping ominously to the left. Ashmole won the cup. The Head at assembly announced that Will had suffered spinal damage and was unlikely to return to school soon. Jim suffered feelings of guilt to his death a year ago. No-one saw Paddy's grip on Will's feet that he'd rapidly released and only when he saw Jim last year he admitted to his involvement.

More of my leisure time was spent with Jackie and less with the boys who were now working. I spent more time studying and conscious of Mum's concerns, part-time working in gardening to supplement the family income. Thoughts turned to a future with Jackie, and I became more concerned with the international scene and how it might prejudice that future.

Reading my Adrian Mole style diaries of the 1950's I came across a couple of paragraphs that were quite lucid and in retrospect probably transmitted the sense of fear about what was in fact a defining event of the last seventy-five years.

An event that has been hair brushed into historical trivia and at the time the significance of which could not have been foreseen, the crowning of Queen Elizabeth, also probably clouded the eyes of most people in Britain. The memory of the Korean War was still fresh in people's memory and although recorded as a war between South and North Korea, countries of divided people, it was an artificial separation after the end of the Second World War; it was in fact a proxy war between the USA supported by the United Nations, and China supported by Russia. The Korean war had not ended, it was just in suspension, and so the general feeling was that the USA had no need to use their nuclear advantage. Clearly etched in peoples' minds was that a single atomic bomb could do so much damage. In 1955, assessing the temperature of world opinion, China was preparing to invade Formosa (today Taiwan), risking only conventional opposition to reclaim what they saw as their territory and the treasures that the Nationalists had taken with them. President Eisenhower, military leader of the defeat of Germany, made it clear that he would use all the means at his disposal to stop the Chinese. He was believed, and to this day the Chinese have only used rhetoric in their claim on the territory. The main outcome was that it induced Russia and later China to speed up their development of the hydrogen bomb and prevented any realistic use of nuclear weapons as a first strike either by or against them. Had Russia been slow in its development of the bomb, there was a certainty that the USA would have taken advantage of their own superiority and we would now be living at best, with a planet polluted by radiation and continuing major power military conflict.

The sense of fear I had expressed in my diary was the possibility of war bringing back earlier experiences that would threaten the rosy future I expected with Jackie.

CHAPTER 3 – HIGHER EDUCATION AND FATE

I entered the A-level examinations for the second time with confidence and was able to take a holiday in my final days at school with Jackie and her family in Cornwall. I returned to find I had passed the necessary examinations, including English Language, to secure a place at Imperial College, University of London, joining the four friends who made it the previous year. The rest of the summer was stress free, working on building sites, earning a labourer's pay, seeing Jackie but with the clouds of anticipation gathering. Jackie, expecting my electing to accept the Birmingham University offer, had enrolled as a student nurse at the Queen Elizabeth Hospital next to the University. October arrived and the old leather suitcase was packed for the start of term in London. Jackie's grandparents lived near Watford, and we arranged to spend two days there before I left for London. A tearful departure for Euston on my way to accommodation in Notting Hill, just across Kensington Gardens from Imperial College. Reunion with the old school mates cheered me up a little: Alan, with whom I shared a room in the accommodation; Jim who lodged with his relations in Balham; Ron and Dave who were in digs in Battersea. Alan and I moved south of the Thames after settling in at college and much of the out of class study was spent in the Battersea Public Library, and Friday night reunions in the local hostelries. The fresher function recruited me to the rugby club and for that first year I played with the college first team.

Imperial College occupied much of the accommodation off Exhibition Road next to the Science Museum and was in three sub-colleges.: engineering in the City and Guilds College, a rambling set of mostly Victorian buildings, similarly the Royal College of Science with the Royal School of Mines in a slightly more modern building opposite the Albert Hall. Initially I would walk from Notting Hill across Kensington Gardens to college but after moving to Battersea, between Lavender Hill and Clapham Common, my daily journey was a forty-five bus to South Kensington and then a walk past the museums. The digs in Battersea were also occupied by two second year chemical engineering students. Alan an anglicized Frenchman and Bernard from Norfolk. We each had separate bedrooms, sharing a bathroom, and using the front room as a study. It worked out well and I stayed there for two years until Alan and Bernard graduated. During the first year I regularly telephoned home, from telephone box to telephone box and to Jackie at the nurses' home. Mrs. Bailey, the landlady, gave up accommodating students at the end of the second year and I moved to Wandsworth into a flat with John Williams – a fellow electrical engineering student. The first-year course for all aspects of Engineering was common, covering mechanical and electrical subjects, with course work involving testing boilers, engines and electrical motors and generators. If you survived the year by passing the end of year examinations and the coursework you were then focused on your chosen engineering discipline. Our classes were in large lecture theatres along narrow corridors and changing floor levels, as buildings had over the years grafted on to the main part. I made friends, whom I stayed connected with and two are still with us. Weekends for that first year were a mixture of exploring London, theatre, concerts, and skiffle in Soho basements with coffee bars, organized by the lads from school who were familiar with the scene. I managed to hitch-hike back to Birmingham to see Jackie and make a fleeting visit home on a couple of times each term. In the 1950s, England was hiker friendly, keeping us hitch-hikers well catered for; keeping teenager's mobile who were doing their national service and impecunious students from working class families. In the latter class to get away from the city to visit home and girlfriend at half term, not carrying heavy luggage. I would get away early on Friday, catch the tube to Edgeware and start to walk north along the Watling Street. I would usually get a lift within half an hour, the lorry driver assuming I was a National Serviceman, asking "Which unit are you with?" After explaining that I was a university student studying engineering, things would go quiet for a while then we would exchange stories, usually about earlier lifts, until we reached my destination in the midlands.

If we survived the first year, we were expected to spend part of our summer working with an engineering company to obtain practical experience. The large electrical companies offered suitable eight-week courses. I arranged with a company near to home, the General Electric Co. The Christmas and Easter breaks were spent living at home but spending a considerable time with Jackie, against Mum's wishes. Apart from the enjoyment, it offered me a taste of living with a different class of people. Her dad, Edgar, was the manager of a branch of a large publishing firm and her mother, privately educated, was a musician. She encouraged me to take Jackie to orchestral concerts in the Birmingham Town Hall.

I survived the first-year examination – quite an accomplishment as the failure rate said to be around forty percent. Before starting the work assignment, I had obtained permission of Jackie's parents for us to take a youth hostelling holiday in the Lake District. Mum and Dad had no objection provided I paid for it myself. Living costs were supported by a local authority grant from which I managed to save a little, and with my labouring wages I could afford to do that (although Dad did help on the quiet). The week before our holiday I was offered a lift home from Jackie's by her dad. I usually walked home, so although curious did accept. Just short of our house he stopped and gave me a Fatherly talk.

Until researching this episode I did not appreciate its significance.

In short, he said he understood the situation with me and Jackie, and that he knew that mature women had desires. He did not explain further except to show that being away at college I should recognize Jackie's plight.

I thought he was warning me to resist sexual intercourse, but I now know that he was implying that resistance could lead to it being looked for elsewhere.

We had a good walking holiday, sleeping in separate dormitories in the youth hostels, our petting taking place in the wild. I sensed a cooling when in a secluded place near Derwent Water and our petting was getting heavy. When invited to go all the way, I declined. We returned home and days later walking in Sutton Park Jackie was very cool and eventually she blurted out that we could not continue and that we should part. She took no pleading. The rest of my placement at GEC was dominated by self-pity. In the lunch breaks I read the life story of Vincent Van Gogh, a sad story that reflected my mood but not leading to self-harm.

Two lessons learned from my brief romance: consideration for another's life and an appreciation of classical music.

Following the placement, I took a labouring job until the commencement of my second year in London. This academic year focused on electrical engineering, power generation, transmission, and electronics, including the recently introduced theory of solid-state components, transistors. I chose to concentrate on the power aspects having seen the potential for work on significant construction projects in my placement with GEC. The course also called for industrial experience in the summer vacation and this time we could seek placement abroad. I applied to work in the Swiss power system. No longer expecting an immediate postgraduate domestic situation, my social activities similarly diverted: playing rugby on Saturdays and often Sundays against the second and third teams of the London clubs. We occasionally played other University teams outside London, the transport leaving from the college. I would arrange to be there early to sit in with the jazz band practicing for the evening dance in the Union. I had become keen on jazz from youth club days where we had a group quite competent in playing traditional jazz. Less time for cultural activities, short-term female friendships from college hops, and skiffle clubs in Soho where teenagers congregated. The academic year was harder and needed more independent study, so many weekday evenings were spent in the library. The year passed quickly, and I survived the end of year examinations.

After a successful year and having experience of the industry the earlier summer I was given the chance this year of experience in a foreign country. I chose to work with a Swiss power company on their hydro-power system. After a brief spell at home and working on the buildings, I flew to Switzerland on a twin-engine turboprop one-way ticket provided by the college, the theory being that I would earn sufficient funds to pay my way back. I was stationed initially in Olten, a small town on the river Aare between Basle and Zurich, to be debriefed and was posted to a hydro power station at Gosgen in the Jura mountains. I lived in the local restaurant and spent my days touring round the power station and practicing my German although it was a mixture of that and English. The local Swiss were not that familiar with High German, although I would hardly call my version that, and spoke a variant Sweitzer-deutch. I returned to Olten to work on technical matters related to the control and stability of the hydro-generators. In Olten I stayed with a family, sharing with an American student also with the power company. The family were keen to have their two children improve their spoken English, whether they did with my Brummy accent, and the American is debatable. Had a two-week spell in a hydro station that was part of a cascade of stations along the river Tessin valley towards Italy. My German language had improved, I stayed in a hotel in Piotino, and was often mistaken by the Italian speaking locals as a German: I grew a moustache and was playfully called Kaiser Wilhelm. At weekends in Olten I would explore the Jura mountains, but hitch-hiking was frowned upon in Switzerland and although there were lifts, they were usually accompanied by rumours of criminal behaviour by the hiker. Wartime memories were fresh – usually tales of crime committed by refugees.

I took a holiday to visit the mountains and lakes in the southern regions by hitching lifts, the route taking me through Bern and then south to the Grimsel Pass. I had little luck at the start with what was mostly holiday traffic, until at the outskirts of Bern a large Mercedes driven by an army officer stopped and offered a lift. After giving the usual lecture about the Swiss attitude to hitchhikers he interrogated me, was satisfied I was not a threat to Switzerland, and enroute gave me a detailed account of the role of the Swiss army. Explaining that it was staffed by every able-bodied male in the country, who after the first term of service had to complete two weeks duty every year. All their gear and equipment were kept at home allowing them to instantly spring to action. In his case, the colonel's uniform, a rifle, machine gun, revolver with ammunition and the Mercedes. He was due to command a battalion guarding an area that included roads, railways and dams forming reservoirs in the high mountains with pipelines to hydro power stations. Stations and dams mined ready to be destroyed, access routes mined, expecting threats from outside. The ease of my travel ended when part way up the pass the car stopped at a narrow side road to turn off and my route was ahead. I started to walk up the steep zig-zagging road. Cars passed laden with luggage for the holiday weekend and no intention of giving a lift, clearly showing the Swiss attitude to hitch-hiking. Following the pass but at a steeper incline was a funicular railway directly to a station at the head. I saw no trains (if there were one it could be detected well ahead) and so I decided to take the direct route, climbing the track. Like a staircase, the sleepers supplied the steps. As the sun went behind the mountains the chilly air caused a fog that left little visibility and as I reached the head of the pass, realised that I would have to stop until daybreak. Out of the fog came a small figure dressed in a greatcoat and asked me if I wanted to stay overnight in a hotel that appeared from the fog. It had an impressive façade and was far beyond my budget. I explained and was told not to worry as they were used to visitors like me that they accommodated in a dormitory in the attic. Eagerly accepting the offer, I found a straw mattress and blanket, and staked a claim on the wooden floor. I had a frugal meal in the bar, with two Germans who were living there for the summer season as photographer and subject. The subject was dressed in a polar bear skin for tourist pictures against the snowy peaks. The following morning, I managed a lift on the back of a fellow student's motor bike to a youth hostel by lake Lucerne.

Returning to Olten by train, I finished my tour of duty and started my way home. I had enough money for the rail fare to Calais and a ferry ticket, but now being confident decided to hitch hike. It was a weekend. The roads were teeming with traffic – mostly German holidaymakers' cars packed with luggage – and I had not learned the lesson. I walked in the direction of Zurich and was clearly not going to get a lift: no sympathetic lorry drivers. I had not spent all my Swiss currency, so when I came to a railway station I gave up and bought a ticket to Dover via Zurich. On the station platform were an English couple looking very bedraggled with a cardboard box full of clothes and oddments. They had been in a car hit by a train on a level crossing and all they recovered was in the cardboard box. On the train I shared my last five franks with them buying frugal snacks. Hitching from Dover (no problem as lorry drivers were looking for company), I arrived back home to surprised parents' days earlier than they expected.

Back to the buildings, accounting the Swiss episodes to my friends in the local pubs and ready for the final year in London. More independent study, writing up the technical aspects of the Swiss assignment, and project work including basic research. Imperial were on the lookout for budding engineering researchers. The rugby season was promising: a French tour in the Christmas holiday but brought to an abrupt stop for me when I broke my leg in a game with a London Welsh team. I spent a week in hospital, then walking with crutches until the Christmas break. Back to the cultural weekends which focused on the London Welsh club and the Guildhall School of Music. My flat mate John from the Welsh valleys was a keen supporter of the London Welsh and was close to one of the lady sopranos at the Guildhall. He thought it would be good therapy for me to watch my oppressors and meet a nice girl.

It promised to be a good game with extramural entertainment. The Welsh had dedicated support including a group of ladies from the Guildhall School of Music populated with large sopranos. The Welsh were winning so it promised to be an entertaining afternoon. Half time and shandies, with speculation about the 'talent' on the touchline and me, being one of the greener members about my virginal state. I overheard a comment from Blodwen, a particularly large lady saying, "they broke his leg, what a shame such a lovely boy." The second half was significantly slower, the match ended with a clear win for the Welsh. After beers in the bar the crowd broke into song: the traditional Welsh choruses, led by the ladies, a discordant male rendering of English 'folk songs' that gravitated to what was known in those far-off days as rugby songs. Blodwen, encouraged by John, moved towards me capturing me between the bar and wall, her body supplying support as strong as any prop-forward. The song, about a Girls School, was in full blast and Blodwen with all her power delivered the final verse that clearly showed her intentions for the rest of the day. As she blasted out the final word John took the initiative and started to sing the Welsh national anthem. A thunderous response from the teams and the lady choristers shook the clubhouse when a lone Englishman, his voice becoming highly pitched and his cheeks becoming redder as each moment passed, gave the final verse. "Wales, Wales bloody great fishes are whales." In the ensuing melee as bottles, glasses, chairs, and tables disintegrated, the clubroom became a heaving mass of bodies. I slid past Blodwen's ample body, slunk to the exit, and escaped.

Most Saturdays were given to playing rugby at the Imperial College ground (on what is now Heathrow airport by the village of Hayes) or away games that we travelled to by coach from the College Union building. We would return in the evening to attend the hop, hoping to attract female company, but were usually unsuccessful after consuming too much beer after the match.

I struggled with the year's project, not being of the inventive mentality, but managed to get a reasonable overall assessment for the degree. Once the demanding work of the year was complete our year of heavy electrical power students organized a tour of manufacturing companies. A dozen, or more, companies were eager to recruit engineers for the work of renewing the broken industrial scene. Building power stations and steelworks for the future. I applied for Graduate Apprenticeships with the companies, travelling and accommodation expenses were covered, and had a week tour of factories in the Midlands, Lancashire, and the Northeast, including a weekend in the Lake District and a visit to the recently commissioned Nuclear Power Station at Calder Hall. We were not aware at the time of the radiation escape from the nearby experimental reactor at Windscale, now Sellafield, but there was no personal injury, in fact we got good exercise walking the hills. We returned to college, faced our final examinations, held our departing celebrations, and left for home. The journey home was on foot. Brother Richard came to London and stayed in my flat in Wandsworth while I packed my belongings to send ahead leaving the bare essential, camping equipment and a change of clothing that we could carry in rucksacks. Taking the underground to join the Grand Union Canal at Tring, we started our trek north. We walked the towpath and stopped to camp overnight, usually near a canal side pub. To Richard's annoyance I would not allow him in the pubs as he was only fourteen. We walked as far as Daventry where our tent could not withstand the downpour and we decided to hitch a lift. A convenient lift took us to the Hardwick Arms at the top of our road. We arrived home to receive notification of the degree results and an invitation to the London University Ceremony in the Albert Hall to be presented with a degree by the Queen Mother. Mum and Dad came with me and met my friends and their parents and enjoyed the pomp of the ceremony and the sights of the city. Back to the building work, further interviews, and choice of employer from three offers. I accepted a Graduate Apprenticeship with the English Electric Company at Stafford.

CHAPTER 4 – PROFESSIONAL TRAINING AND FIRST REAL JOB.

Before starting work with the English Electric Company, I had a medical. The GP was concerned about my blood pressure being high, gave me pills that had no effect, and sent me to see a consultant. On checking, the consultant said he found no problem and explained that the doctor had seen the White Coat Syndrome that people live with. A flight or fight reaction that sensitive people show. On receiving the consultant's report, the doctor gave me a clean bill of health.

I still have the condition and can very easily be startled by the sound of a penny dropping.

Rather than travel daily to Stafford I took lodgings so that I could keep up with the social side of the area. Initially I had a bed breakfast and evening meal lodging five days of the week returning home for the weekends. The widowed proprietor lived with her middle-aged son who worked in the contract office at the EE Co. Later, three of us on the same course rented a house, John who was also at I.C. and Dudley who played the trumpet.

The first week of the apprenticeship was an initiation with lectures about the company and its history. We then had a series of training lectures covering management subjects such as quality control, production control, planning, and metallurgy. The instruction was in the education department and in the Stafford Technical College. We had to do practical training in the use of machine tools alongside the student and craft apprentices. The training programme, over two years, was geared to give practical experience of the complete range of disciplines necessary to run a design and manufacturing organisation. As graduates we were already well versed in the technical aspects, so our stay was less than the students and craft apprentices in training for longer periods. Everyone spent time in welder training supervised by a likeable individual called Sammy who made sure we could recognise good welding and do it ourselves. The company's products included fabricated structures held together by welds: generators, switchgear, transformers, electric motors, and control panels of all sizes. We spent time on the shopfloor in the departments that covered the manufacture and then in the design and drawing offices. The large machines were balanced in the High Bay of the style which was familiar to me from my first vacation training with GEC two years earlier. During the two years we were expected to spend a month on a construction site where the Outside Department were installing equipment, taking part in its test, and commissioning. I spent five weeks at the South Durham Steelworks that was under construction on a green field site. The Works built to make steel plate for a shipyard on the Tyne. Lodged in Seaton Carew near West Hartlepool shared accommodation with structural steel workers who were building the mill housings. Our company supplied the drives and controls for the plate mill including the roller tables and the shears and cooling tables. Given the job of checking the installation of the electric motors, supplies, and controls, while the senior commissioning engineer was overall responsible and took it on himself to check the main drive, a fifty thousand horsepower motor and controls and roll adjusting drives for the screw-downs. Having showed that I was familiar with electronics, I was handed the task of commissioning an electronic computer to programme the operation of the screw-downs. I later found out I had deprived a specialist from Stafford having days on site. I saw the mill enter operation rolling red-hot ingots into plate and spent weeks on standby in case of faults in the power and control systems. Returning to Stafford to complete my apprenticeship, I joined the Institution of Electrical Engineers as a member.

I was now familiar with the ways I could gain a profession in electrical engineering in design of equipment, manufacturing management, research, installation, and commissioning. I could not see how my wider interest in large projects could be satisfied. The building of steelworks was designed, planned and their construction managed by the owner, the Nationalised steel company. As were power stations by the Central Electricity Board.

During my time in Stafford, I spent the evenings socialising at the apprentice club that had a bar and games room and was open to all the grades of apprentice that included women who were also allowed to bring in their friends, particularly on Fridays when we usually had a band and dancing. At weekends I would travel home via Lichfield to play rugby and spend Sunday with Mum, Dad, Jill (a trainee nurse in Walsall), Pat, Carole, and Richard, who were at secondary school. Sunday evenings were often spent at a local pub with the lads still at home with their girlfriends. I would return to Stafford early Monday. I met Jean who was for a brief spell my companion, but the association was interrupted.

With my keenness to join the Commissioning Department noted, I was posted to India for the last five months of my course to help commission a Rod and Bar Mill at the Indian Iron and Steel Works in Burnpur, West Bengal. I was promised a position with the department on return and while away a forty percent salary increase: an opportunity I could not resist and so I succumbed to a medical examination and the right vaccinations. It was a given that my first overseas job was a new greenfield development in West Bengal, a consortium engineered steelworks near Asansol Junction, the model for a John Master's novel, *Bhowani Junction*.

In the company surgery. It was only a little prick, but I shook with fear as I heard the hiss of the hypodermic needle. I hated pain, particularly when bent forward with trousers around my knees. This was the first of a series of injections for travel to a tropical climate. My first time out of Europe, first time on a jet engined Comet 4. At each refuelling stop the temperature and humidity increased and when, what seemed like a lifetime later, the doors opened at Dum-Dum Airport, Calcutta, the hot humid air entered the cabin instantly raising the atmosphere to that of a hothouse. The temperature in the shade was 102 degrees. I had only ever experienced this temperature and humidity when accidently locked in a tomato greenhouse as a child.

Was met by a colleague, Max, guided through immigration and customs after releasing part of the duty-free goodies into unofficial hands, and off to the hotel through almost impenetrable streets of Kolkata (Calcutta), populated by heaving masses of humankind and meandering cows. A quick shower, shopping for tropical clothes and to Firpo's the local expat meeting place. The first question after handing out the goodies, "how long are you here for?" Raucous laughter when I replied, "only two months" and met with a selection of durations, one of which was, "since before the war as initially movement was restricted and then I liked it" without explaining further but, he knew local ladies. Next morning, after a restless night wafted by the Punka-fan, I experienced a crowded train-ride through bright green paddy fields, scanty forests, bright red flame of the forest blossom, isolated thatched villages and watering stages with platforms teeming with humanity, hoping the train would pause long enough to grab hold and climb to the roof. Comfortable in our airconditioned reserved carriage it was all a little remote. Finally, to the junction town, Asansol, where I was collected by a Willey's Jeep to the Guest House, a feature of the British Raj to accommodate temporarily incoming families and special occasions. Into the dhobi went the sweat sodden tropical gear, a shower, into another set of the half a dozen outfits bought in Kolkata (Calcutta) and off to the Resident Engineer's bungalow to meet the rest of the crew, once more ridiculed about my expected time in the territory.

I was collected early, while comparatively cool, and off to the steelworks, a site similar to those locations in the UK, from Port Talbot to Hamilton, but a little warmer. The project was to commission a steel rod and bar mill, the installation being complete. A furnace for heating steel billets, four-inch square and twelve foot long, that when heated to a plum red are pushed into a series of rolling stands and successively reduced and manipulated to a final round section one inch diameter. To accommodate the increased length of steel approximately two hundred feet long, the billet would start its journey through twelve roller stands in a line, then the steel having increased length and speed was to be guided through a further six parallel stands to a cutting machine, a flying shear, chopped into twelve-foot lengths with the steel travelling at sixty miles an hour, then transferred to a cooling bed. The tricky part of this process is for the rollers to precisely shape, reduce and keep the rod in a line to enter the next roller stand. The roller speed of each stand adjustable by a controller to match the increasing speed of steel. Fairly straightforward until at the exit from the twelfth stand the speeding steel was to be directed into a guide that turns it through 180 degrees into the parallel two stands, then that must be repeated a further two times sending the rod to the flying shear. The shear was controlled to meet the sixty miles per hour rod exiting the eighteenth stand to cut it without causing an obstacle. Not easy to describe but even less easy to achieve with a brand-new setup.

The main job was to ensure that all the motors, cabling, control systems, protection and instrumentation were installed correctly, and that the motors ran smoothly, driving the roller stands through the correct speed range to the operator's requirements. A month was spent in basements in the high humidity and then attendance while the steel was threading through the mill. Success was achieved stand by stand, with frequent cobbles as the rod did not enter the next stand, sending a speeding snake of red-hot material into the rafters. This stage was endless and right up to the opening day, steel did not travel as far as the flying shear. On one occasion the roller man, whose job was to check the profile of the steel rod, stood astride the speeding snake to burn the steel profile onto a hardwood staff, and was trapped in a cage of cobbled red-hot steel at the final stand. He managed to withstand the heat, remaining stock still while with the help of the overhead crane and oxy acetylene cutters the cage lifted away.

The official opening was to be by the chairman of the steel company, Sir Biren Mukherjee with the Minister of Industry, and officials. They were to arrive at an auspicious time, when things went right, Mid-day on the Saturday. So far steel had still not threaded right through the mill. Being a Saturday, the normal working start time was an inauspicious time, when things were more likely to go wrong, and with the roller man recognising he should not defy the fates, and needing all the time he could get, he arranged to start two hours earlier at 3.30 am. The rod smoothly travelled to just short of the flying shear where it stubbornly coiled on the mill floor and in the rafters. By eleven a.m. the roller man stopped rolling and cleared the cobbled steel. Reporters from Kolkata Times had been around throughout the morning busy taking extensive shots of the chaos. What more to do but to hope that by avoiding the inauspicious hour to start, and opening at an auspicious time the Gods would be pleased?

Sir Biren's Rolls Royce arrived followed by the Minister and entourage, greeted by the Managing Director of the steelworks, and guided to the control pulpit overlooking the array of a pristine rod mill and stood behind four controllers in front of a desk of eighteen sets of speed controls. The roller man stood in front of the mill. The lead controller was given the ok to start and sounded a high-pitched horn. The steel billet appeared from the furnace, threaded through the first stand, the controller adjusted the roll speed then as the speeding steel worked its way through successive stands the control was passed along to the first 180 degree turn through the next and the next, and approached the flying shear at a speed undetectable to the eye. The operator at the shear control point cut the rod relying entirely on the operationally untested control to do its job. Successively six billets were rolled, and the cooling beds, only previously proved with cold steel, filled with slowly cooling rod. Sir Biren shook hands with all concerned and left with his entourage. Hardly had the official cars left the site when the next billet found its way to the shear and left for the rafters. Back to chaos that lasted on and off for the next two weeks until a stable output was achieved. The following Monday's Kolkata newspaper had a full page of both the chaos and success, describing in flowery language the hellish scene only cured by the God-like presence of Sir Biren.

A successful handover. I was on call for a month and after handing over to our Indian engineers and the customer's engineers I was ready to leave. Technically still a trainee who had to be properly appointed, I was due to return home; however, I was approached by the Site Manager and told that before returning home I was to report to the General Manager at Durgapur, a green field project to supply and build a steelworks by a consortium of nine British companies. He explained that the commissioning engineer Bill, in charge of EECO extent of work, was due for home leave and he needed cover during that period, only another two months. Bill and I got on well, his home leave was not due for a couple of months and in the meantime, he made sure I was aware of the full extent of the work, both completed and still to do. Bill familiarized me with the project overall that was for a completely new Steelworks taking raw materials, iron ore, coal and limestone mined close by to convert it into iron, steel and to fabricate it by forging, and rolling into construction steel products, railway wheels and strip for car bodies to make manufacturing in India self-supporting. The contract for the design, supply and construction was financed by a long term, low interest loan guaranteed by the British

Government and implemented by a consortium of nine British companies one of which was EE Co. who supplied the 11 KV switchgear, the 440 Volt distribution system, the drives and controls for the Billet Mill and the controls for three Blast Furnaces. Bill also familiarized me with the local area, which I had not had the chance to appreciate while at Burnpur, the social side of the camp introducing me to the other English company engineers, and the Mython Dam sailing club where we were welcome to hire dinghies at the weekends. I was beginning to become suspicious of his involving me for what was a noticeably short stay, when he confided that he was not going to return and that he hoped the General Manager would explain to me that I was his replacement for the rest of the project, expected to be up to two years. Accustomed to working in India and the challenge of the responsibility was one I was happy to take on. When I saw the Manager and he explained the circumstances I said I was prepared to take on the role, provided the Head Office agreed and that I would first return home to complete the formalities of completing the apprenticeship and taking up full time employment with the company. After checking with the Company Director in Kolkata who confirmed that Stafford agreed, he arranged my ticket home.

I returned to Stafford and debriefed, received my certificate of apprenticeship, and officially joined the Outside Department as a Commissioning Engineer, an improved salary and collected my air ticket to Kolkata after two weeks holiday. I tidied up my things in the flat, had a night out with the lads and Jean, who I had stayed connected with. Jean was a little cool towards me and I found out from the lads that she had been dating the son of one of the managers. After spending the two weeks at home with the family and the friends who were still in the area, I was then away again –this time with no allusions as to the length of time I would be away.

I was welcomed by the Manager, reunited with Bill, the Indian Engineers, Mukherjee, Sinha, Sen Gupta and Goswamy and the

Forman, Gordon an Anglo-Indian. Bill then passed over the records that included the details of the plant handed over to the customer and the outstanding work given to the engineers. My role was management, technical supervision and customer contact with the occasional problem solving particularly with the computer interface. I was allocated a bungalow accommodation that I shared with a chemical engineer who managed the commissioning of the oxygen plant on the project. We had a servant, Ali Jan, who with the cook and gardener kept us fed and tidy. Ali was a Muslim and in the dominant Hindu population was often concerned about his safety. Weekends and short breaks were the opportunity for me to visit Kolkata, New Delhi, The Tajh Mahal at Agra, and a trip to visit the Hydro Electric Station near Amritsar, where EE Co were installing the generators and electrical systems. The engineer there was my supervisor, Colin, when I was at South Durham.

I familiarized myself with the surrounding villages, driving a company Jeep as I had managed to get an Indian driving license with the help of the Engineers' local knowledge. Over Christmas holiday the Manager took a holiday in Hong Kong and left me in charge. I lived in his house and used his Studebaker with the engineers to go on visits of local interest. The Manager had been a dockyard commander in Hong Kong after the war and was regularly to recount his association with the Governor, Lord Mountbatten he called Dickie, to the ridicule of the regulars behind his back at the club bar.

The Queen and Duke of Edinburgh took time out of their busy visit to India in 1961 to visit the Durgapur Steel Works. We were given a days' notice of the visit and invited to a reception in the gardens of the Club. Required to wear formal dress, I did not have a dinner jacket but recommended having my bearer, Ali Jan, contact a local tailor. A tailor arrived at the bungalow armed with glossy brochures showing men in different forms of suit. We selected the style, explained the finer points like the barathea lapels of the jacket and the seams of the trousers. The tailor took my measurements and promised to bring the suit for fitting the following day, the reception being in the evening. An anxious day but the tailor and suit turned up on time. It was a good fit but the whole of the jacket was made from barathea, giving it a shiny gloss. It was too late to remake it so I wore the outfit and as we assembled lining the path the Royal entourage would take, I felt a little exposed. The Royal Couple approached our section of the line-up stopping to speak to a choice of people. As they came close, I will swear The Queen was about to approach me when the flash of a camera on the opposite side lit up my jacket, and she moved on. I was the source of amusement later in the bar.

Working on a single project site and living close to the other workers, professionals, and management of nine British firms allowed for a better understanding of the project overall and the platform for discovering how things work. This was a tremendous advantage, although not recognised at the time.

Entertainment in the remote location was the club bar, the weekly Housey-housey (Bingo) sessions and Saturday Tiffin lunches if you were invited. Nothing like the life of adventure with the James Bond image. The lack of single female company meant that evenings in the club bar were populated with roving expatriate males who had been stuck in India and other Asian locations since before the second world war and were not shy about how they exercised their sexual desires or their other escapades. The late-night drinking sessions were beginning to become a habit and my association with a clique of inveterate characters was noticed by the Welsh wife of the senior electrical engineer, who made it clear to me that this lifestyle was not doing me any good. That and an episode escorting one of the clique, who had imbibed one too many, back to his bungalow retching and loudly singing unrepeatable rugby songs, upset the neighbours, and led to a formal complaint. It caused me to rethink the plan to lead the life of a roaming bachelor. Clearly, if I were to continue with my ambition to lead a large overseas project, I would have to choose a more stable private life. At a Tiffin lunch I was taken to one side by the senior electrical engineer and advised that if I wanted to pursue this style of career, I would be more stable with a family and that for large, long-term projects companies expected that managers have partners.

When the work was complete and the Indian engineers capable of supplying the standby, I was released to return home in May 1961. I returned home significantly lighter and wiser but suffering from persistent diarrhoea. I found myself once again in the company surgery. This time I was issued with a small bottle, corked with spatula and little instruction other than, "Bring it back with a sample." On consulting the shopfloor, I was advised to "Just fill it up and spoon out the excess with the spatula." The best advice of the whole episode. I debriefed to the Commissioning Manager and left the works for my leave.

On the way home, wealthier than a year or so ago, I visited a motor car salesroom and bought a new pale blue Morris Mini for £450.00 and drove home. I spent the holiday with family sharing a bedroom to my brother's concern, renewing old contacts, and showing off my new car. With the ability to travel freely I drove to Stafford after my break and reported for duty.

The Commissioning manager had a position to fill at the Steel Company of Wales. I spent a week in the rectifier department as this Temper Mill was the first to be powered by direct current produced by a transformer rectifier. Then, posted to the Cardiff branch where I was briefed and dispatched to Port Talbot to take on the commissioning of the Temper Mill at the large Steelworks of British Steel. The Steel strip, coiled and cooled after it had been rolled by the strip rolling mill, now had to be finished using the stretching and slight reduction in thickness to be a suitable quality for car bodies, achieved by tempering when passing through this mill. The site manager, Hugh, was about to leave having seen the bulk of the plant and electrics installed. We reviewed the outstanding installation work with the supervisor and agreed that Hugh would stay to see the bulk of that work while I reviewed the information and test gear needed for the test and commissioning. I found accommodation above a pub in Porthcawl and contacted my old friend Ray who had a house in Swansea and was preparing to get married to Barbara in September. I also contacted John, my college friend who was married to Rhiannon and lived in Neath. In charge of the site once Hugh left, I prepared to start up the supplies finding a defect in the rectifier transformer that could not be fixed on site and arranged with the Cardiff office for its dispatch back to Stafford. It was found to have a winding fault, and while waiting for its return with a replacement winding with the help of David an engineer from the Cardiff office, we started to check the circuitry and power connections to the motors and control systems. Dick, an engineer released from the site in Ebbw Vale, joined us and we began pre-start up checks so that we were ready to power the plant when the transformer returned two weeks later.

Another lesson learned: do not let the responsible person leave until secure in the knowledge that installation is proven to be sound.

The power supplies and control systems were set up, tested and ready to run the motors; initially disconnected from the load all went well and ready to run connected to the loads. Here we met with a problem with a motor connected to the flexible drive shaft of the mechanism that supplied the tension on the strip. The motor was badly aligned and had damaged the commutator. We were faced with another failure: the motor had to have the commutator skimmed and we had to call back the installation engineer to align the machine with the motor. All then went well, and we were ready to hand over to the customer's operational crew to set up the process. A coil of rolled strip steel was loaded on the input side of the main drive, the strip threaded through the main rollers and connected to the tension coiler, the main rollers were screwed to pinch the strip to reduce it by a defined amount and the main drive started synchronized with the speed of the un-coiler providing tension in the strip the coiler drive synchronized to the tension required pulling the strip into a finished coil. This complex process required days of setting up including analysis of the finished product to satisfy specification. Finally, production that included managing the coils and storing the finished product was achieved and the mill ready for orders. We had a standby role until the customers electrical engineers were confident all outstanding, so-called defects, were corrected. The progress of the commissioning halted during an industrial action by the steelworkers' union which caused shutdown of the complete steelworks lasting three weeks. During this period, I was given other tasks, mine being to help the commissioning of a tinning line at the SCOW in Ebbw Vale at Tredegar.

CHAPTER 5 – SETTLING DOWN.

During my time in South Wales, I met with Ray and Barbara and often joined them with their friends at a country club, The Langrove near Swansea. I was invited to their wedding where, at the reception Barbara introduced me to Myra. We got on well, both being in our late twenties, and arranged to date. On Saturdays I met John, my old college mate, to play golf and even bought a half set of clubs. Myra and I continued to date and when invited to Sunday lunch, I met her Mum, Hilda, at her home in Banwell Street, Morriston, and enjoyed Hilda's cooking and entertainment with tales of the past. Myra's Dad Ernest Jones died the previous year. I met Myra's Brother and family in the army stationed in Penzance living in army quarters, discovering that our families had experienced similar early years.

Ernest had worked at Stewarts and Lloyds steelworks in Morriston. His job at the mill face was to catch the dull red plate in steel tongues as it exited the rollers and send it back through the three-high, plate mills. He would return home to Hilda and seven-year-old David usually physically exhausted. Hilda at 35 was heavily pregnant with Myra and not liking it, the public house was more relaxing for Ernest. In May his horizon changed with the birth of Myra, a dark haired beautiful little girl and he signed the pledge. The next four years were filled with tension building up to World War, and then the austerity of war and the slow recovery. Ernest had served in the First World War at both the battle of the Somme and in Gallipoli and returned to his essential job at the steelworks. In the Second World War the Swansea docks and the manufacturing factories were bombed on a nightly basis with high damage to residential areas. The small terraced two-up that Ernest's family occupied spared. Myra got the attention from her dad that few of her schoolmates with their dads in the army were fortunate enough to get.

At the very beginning of the war Ernest took Myra to the local council school. The industrial part of South Wales where coal and iron mining had taken over large swathes of the workforce was populated by English speaking people who had emigrated from the South-West of England that had a surplus workforce, redundant from the fall off in demand during the depression where demand for tin, copper, lead, and iron in Cornwall had been a massive industry. In Cornwall Devon and Dorset there was China clay; stone in Somerset; Portland stone in Dorset and limestone in Gloucestershire. Labour was harvested from those areas to follow their trades in coal mining, steel making and support industries. In the depression, families from the mining areas in the South-West moved to South Wales resulting in large families living in and around Morriston. Myra's birth was remarkable: Hilda was thirty-five, past the age recognised in those days as safe for bearing children. Ernest was older and seen to have done his duty in the earlier war, so Myra was a glimmer of hope and a jewel particularly in her father's eye.

Myra and I grew up in similar circumstances, but our paths did not cross for nearly three decades. Now in my mid-eighties I am looking to leave a record of my lifetime which would be as nothing without Myra. One promise we made when it seemed our future together would be inevitable was that since we both had interesting lives, we would keep aspects of them to ourselves and not probe into sensitive past.

Myra's early years can be pieced together from photographs from family records, stories that come from remaining relatives, stories from her school and work mates and sheer speculation. For the circumstances surrounding life of their generation, it can be taken as like that of mine which is to a significant extent recorded and remembered.

Apart from luck, what is it that brings together two people in a lasting relationship? In general, it is tied to the experiences of early life when character forming aspects are experienced. Naturally, a common development will draw people together, that is, the environment. The environment is primarily the close family relationships and attitudes as well as the general circumstances.

While there was not a pressing need to learn Welsh, Ernest made efforts to grasp the basics of the language that he saw as a poetic one, not as was assumed at the time a dead one. This and his intent to study English grammar gave Myra an interest in language, poetry and particularly the writings of Dylan Thomas. Hilda was a short, stout lady, prone to obesity that added to the stress of bearing a child in her mid-thirties, exaggerated by the prolapsed uterus that developed following the birth. Hilda could be outspoken and was not shy in blaming both Earnest and Myra for her predicament. The effect was to make Earnest more protective of his daughter and as she grew, proud of her achievements, encouraging her through the years of scarcity and as normality returned interesting her in the rugby of the area, particularly the Swansea team with regular visits to the St. Helens ground to see the Whites play. Regular Sunday visits to see his relatives gave him the excuse of a pint with his brother, and for Myra to amuse the aunts whose families had grown up and those with husbands away at war.

Myra grew to be taller than the average for her age which earned respect of the children at school, but also a certain amount of teasing. The primary school for Morriston was flattened in the air raids of 1941 and so over a year of formal education was lost that resulted in loss of learning that Ernest did his best to remedy for Myra. None of the pupils at the school passed the 11-plus examination that was created in the Education Act of 1944 to give children a place at the Grammar School. The secondary modern schools, Myra knew would not satisfy her view of a future and she made that clear to her parents. Ernest decided to pay for private education, although it would be a financial struggle, and Myra completed her education at a secretarial college. While providing a step up, it did not satisfy her desire for higher education, but gave that first rung on the career ladder with a job in the typing pool at Stewarts and Lloyds. Myra was an avid reader and took every opportunity of technical school to achieve certification and responsibility as well as making lifetime girlfriends. She gained confidence while missing the opportunity to go to university; nevertheless, she gained the position of head of the typing pool and the experience of management that allowed her to move to the new factory of Imperial Metals, where initially she joined the personnel department, became Secretary to the Construction Manager and then Head of the Secretarial Services Department and Secretary to Head of Commercial Department. Finally, Myra became Secretary to Senior Executive of Imperial Chemical Industries Limited in the South Wales Plant where she helped recruit other female professionals. Apart from the academic and social aspects, she had not lost that much from missing university and gained much more practical and business confidence. With her girlfriends she joined the badminton club and helped by her height she became a serious player in both female and mixed competitions. The only evidence of male friendships was companionship and family friends influenced by her dad's strong character and physique. The girls were regulars at the Mumbles Pier dance hall on Saturday nights, catching the last bus to Morriston that deterred other than the keenest of suitors.

As overseas travel became popular, the girls' arranged holidays in the sun at Spanish resorts and on the Mediterranean islands where they met groups of lads, but none seemed to blossom for Myra. Social life began to expand as Saturday nights, moving from the dance hall to gatherings a local country club, sometimes simply having a drink (usually a Babycham) and sometimes a more formal dinner dance, accompanied by a male badminton partner or a work colleague. Myra's dad Earnest had died the year before we met. Myra mortgaged the house at Banwell Street for her to live with Hilda.

Myra and I got on well but with the contract complete at Port Talbot, I was transferred to RTB Scunthorpe to help commission a Billet Mill where Bill, who I took over from at Durgapur, was in charge. I missed Myra while away and mindful of the advice given at Durgapur about lifestyle and having learned from experience about extended periods of absence, I promised to come back to Swansea on my free weekends and Ray and Barbara would accommodate me. A routine of Saturday night cinema, taking Myra and Hilda to visit the beaches of the Gower peninsular with Sunday lunch at Banwell Street, the evening spent at the Langrove Club with our friends. I would return Myra and after a short sleep set off back to Yorkshire.

At RTB Scunthorpe the Billet Mill drives were supplied by direct current from rectifiers, previously supplied by alternating current, driven direct current generators. This was a new development which I had been trained to commission, so I was given that role with Peter L to help me. The project went well, and once it was producing billets, I was transferred to a project on a greenfield site at Ravenscraig near Motherwell in Scotland that was to supply steel strip for the budding car manufacturing in the area. My monthly commute to Swansea continued. The project carefully checked as it had wide economic interests, so sometimes it was difficult to get away. Myra visited once, I met her at Glasgow rail station, and we had a holiday along the West Coast, walking in the hills and staying in a small hotel. We took a long weekend in London staying in a small hotel in Kensington and a summer holiday in Salcombe where we hired a small dingy to explore the coastline. Showing off the sailing skill I had gained on the Maithon Dam in India, proudly I took the tiller, raised the mainsail, and tried to steer away from the quayside. A strong wind filled the sail but no movement. After amusement from the onlookers a smiling angler said, "Best to lower the centreboard," I did and the dingy headed out into the bay. We had a memorable holiday and more scrapes.

Myra agreed to my proposal of marriage. Her mother and my

parents were happy and after that I stayed at Banwell Street in the spare room at weekends. One weekend I arranged for Myra to stay at my home in Streetly to meet my family where she shared the bedroom with my two sisters Pat and Carol, Jill living in the nurses' home at Walsall, while I shared with Richard. The inquisition at the table for Sunday lunch was revealing. Following that, Myra spent weeks at the ICI plant near Birmingham by arrangement with her Chief Executive to help reorganise the Secretarial Services in the Whitton plant and stayed with the family in Streetly.

My role at Ravenscraig was like the earlier projects but on this project, as it was much larger with over thirty engineering staff, the company supplied accommodation. With a commercial manager in charge, I was more constrained, although I was given responsibility for commissioning the main drives. The commissioning phase at Ravenscraig was nearing an end and I asked Jim the Chief Commissioning Engineer in Stafford if he could find me a project with a longer timescale as I was getting married in September 1963 and wanted to take Myra with me to the next project. I spoke at the right time as he was being asked to transfer commissioning engineers to the EE Co. Nuclear Division, Reactor Equipment Department to become accustomed with the standard and style of work and procedures required by the nuclear industry. It satisfied both my need for stability (as the project was likely to last for five years) and my wish to get involved in a separate set of disciplines. I was accepted, and in May 1963, transferred to the Test Facility of EE CO. Reactor Equipment Division in Whetstone, Leicestershire.

CHAPTER 6 – ATOMIC POWER

In the spring of 1963, I joined the Reactor Equipment Division (RED) in Whetstone, Leicestershire, on the site of Frank Whittle's the jet engine development. The site encompassed the gas turbine manufacturing of English Electric, Reactor Equipment Division, the development laboratories and the nuclear consortium, the Atomic Power Division, which included the overall nuclear project management team of EECo, Babcock and Wilcox, boiler makers, and Taylor Woodrow, civil engineers.

This gave me the opportunity to see – as part of the team – the workings of an integrated project from early days.

Over eight thousand employees worked on the site. RED had a test facility that housed a full-scale section of a reactor core used to develop and assess the equipment for loading nuclear fuel elements and could work under pressure to simulate reactor conditions. The reactors were being built and planned for Hinckley Point, Sizewell, and Wylfa Magnox reactors powering 400-megawatt steam turbines. Magnox was the metallic cladding of the elements that held the nuclear fuel. The fuel was loaded into vertical holes in the graphite core of the reactor contained in a steel pressure vessel, pressurized to 400 psi. Our task was to assure by assessing the refuelling machine on a rig with a pressurised vessel and section of simulated reactor core that this could be achieved successfully on the power station. Once satisfied that the equipment was working to specification, I and my colleagues would leave for Sizewell to ensure it was installed and satisfactorily used to load the fuel and to see it run with the reactor at power. This latter phase being similar in function to the commissioning of steelworks, but with an added dimension of concerns about the escape of radiation and the need for assurance that everything was to specification to achieve an operating license. Commissioning documentation, in contrast with control gear in a non-nuclear plan, required an explanation of the function of the mechanism being driven and controlled. This was new compared with non-nuclear applications: at the time, a set of drawings was sufficient for a trained commissioning engineer to work out how to check out a conventional system. Nuclear safety needed written procedures drawn up and approved by the control engineers who often did not have the practical experience of the machinery. Quality procedures required such activities seen and recorded. This was an area to which I could add practical experience and make significant improvements.

Early in my spell at Whetstone, RED became a separate company within English Electric headed by an enigmatic Managing director: hard swearing and drinking ex-Atomic Energy Authority Irishman, Everett Long. I and my fellow engineers from other units were transferred from the Outside Departments of EECo. We came under the Construction department led by John Mowat, a wily Scott. My first job from him was to interview recruits to the department who would go on to help commission the equipment at Sizewell that included all the reactor control and instrumentation, as well as all the fuel handling and loading systems on the two reactors. Additionally, he listened to my concerns about the cumbersome way that test and commissioning schedules were created by designers. After manoeuvring within the new company, he secured the work and gave it to me to organize the commissioning engineers to compile test procedures, using information from the design offices and sending them to Quality department for review and then to clear with the project team and the customer. Together with helping to set to work the fuelling equipment in the test facility, this was a significant job that included the mechanical engineers who also contributed to the commissioning documentation.

During this time, I lived at my parents' home visiting old friends and at weekends I travelled to Swansea and stayed at Myra's enjoying food and entertainment. I had the opportunity to meet her friends and relatives and we usually joined Ray and Barbara and their group at the Landgrove Club on Sunday evening. We planned to have our wedding reception at the club after our marriage in the Llangevelach Church in Swansea. The details of organizing it all I left for Myra and Hilda, as they were far more competent than me.

In Whetstone, the company had a welfare officer who helped me to arrange married accommodation. He secured a flat on an estate used to house US flight crew during the war, taken over by EECo to help with the recruitment and relocation of engineers. I took possession and one weekend Myra visited to decide what furniture we needed for the two-bedroom apartment close to the office in the small village of Cosby. The following week I took time and bought the basic items for delivery before leaving for my annual holiday and wedding.

Arriving in Swansea early on the Friday I collected my morning suit from Moss Bros. and had a clean shave at a barbers shop the following morning, arranged by Ray. I cannot remember the evening. I am told I behaved, but the shave sobered me up and before I knew I was waiting at the Llangevelach Church. Oblivious of the activities and conversations between friends and families waiting in the churchyard, reflecting on our journey together I had a vision of that first date with Myra waiting on the steps of the Dragon Hotel, tall and graceful. Our courtship from then on, albeit fragmented by my travelling to the industrial sites for weeks on end, was positive with no doubts we were to spend our lives together. Myra arrived with long flowing white dress and veil accompanied by her brother Howard, surrounded by both families and friends, we met at the altar. We tied the knot and were transported to the Landgrove Club for the reception with the guests, and thanks to Myra's organizational skill all went like clockwork. We left for our honeymoon in Southern Ireland, staying in Wales for a couple of nights to enjoy the Gower and staying at the Worms Head Hotel where we tied the knot. We took the car ferry from Holyhead and then spent two weeks to slowly take the coast road to Kerry and return overland, stopping to hike in the mountains and staying in local hotels. On return we stayed with Hilda for two days and then to our flat in Cosby.

Back to work and to prepare this massive, shielded mechanism to prove its ability to manage nuclear fuel. No longer a long drive of thirty miles each evening, Myra and I had time to explore the area and to meet my friends and enjoy proper home cooked food and entertainment. Myra soon found a job as a secretary in a small local firm and life took on a settled pace. It was not long before Myra was pregnant and knowing that we arranged to visit Suffolk to find suitable housing near the project. The visit coincided with my trips to the site to prepare for the test and commissioning phase. We settled on a two bedroomed new build bungalow in the small market town of Halesworth about ten miles from the Sizewell site. It would be available in May of 1964 which suited our plans to move shortly after the baby's birth and to move my base to the power station. Annie was born in June in a local maternity hospital. Hilda came from Swansea to nurse Myra when discharged. I managed to convince the sister in the hospital that I could see the birth and fortunately the ward was free of other births at the time. The nurse made me wash and tog-up, worried what she would inflict if I were to faint, and gave me the job of helping with the painkilling gas. Annie delivered without problem. After a few days in hospital Myra returned to our temporary accommodation and I could focus working in the context of a large integrated project.

The customer for the twin four hundred Mwe Sizewell Nuclear Power Station was the Central Electricity Generating Board (CEGB) and the project coordinated by the consortium of the three supply companies who later became a separate company British Nuclear Design and Construction (BNDC). The design, manufacture, and installation of mechanical, reactor and electrical equipment was by the various specialist companies of EECo, the steel fabrication was by B&W and civil works by Taylor Woodrow.

We moved to our new two-bedroom bungalow in Halesworth in September, and I moved my desk to the site office at Sizewell. I met the crew that included engineers that had been transferred from Stafford, like myself, and new recruits who oversaw the installation and testing various parts of the reactor electrical systems, controls, and instrumentation to prepare for operation and system commissioning. Each engineer was familiar with their system as they had been involved in the production of the test documentation. I answered to the EECo, RED, Construction Manager and the senior electrical engineer and oversaw the management of the test and commissioning engineers and for the interface with the project team and customer's inspectors as well as visiting specialists from Whetstone and suppliers. At the time, the RED Construction Manager was resident at Sizewell with a deputy, a mechanical engineer who headed a crew of engineers responsible for building the graphite core of the reactor, installing reactor equipment including the fuelling machinery. The steel pressure vessel shell of the reactor, supplied and fabricated by Babcock and Wilcox of Renfrew, was surrounded by a meter thick reinforced concrete shield wall completed. Installation of the graphite had started under strict, clean conditions to keep stray materials from the volume. The power station formed two reactors; each would supply carbon dioxide, heated to four hundred degrees centigrade by the nuclear reaction, to four steam generators to power the turbines. The first reactor shell was completed, and the turbines installed.

There were familiar faces among the engineers from encounters on other sites, much friendly rivalry, and a good social life. Myra soon made friends and contacts in Halesworth and got on well with the wives and families of my colleagues who were mostly long-term residents for the contract. We took advantage of the beaches at Southwold and Aldborough, the latter town having a cinema and concert hall. Still in contact with friends made at that time. We had no shortage of visitors, including my family and Myra's mum. Howard and family came to stay before emigrating to Adelaide in Australia.

The equipment was installed and set to work, but not without problems. All was resolved to the satisfaction of the inspectorate and the customer but involved more meetings and discussions than I had ever experienced in the steel industry. Gradually the reactor equipment was used to prove to the overall commissioning team and to train the customer's operators so that the reactor could be pressurized to operating temperature and then heated to prove its ability to hold pressure, and then to show the refuelling process using dummy fuel elements. Once it was seen that fuel could be loaded and removed remotely, the nuclear fuel elements were loaded by hand, that being quicker as the fuel elements were handleable before being irradiated, the natural uranium only mildly radioactive. The radiation level on the element when unirradiated is safe and so hand loading was quicker than using the refuelling equipment. The instrumentation for radiation detection and measurement, the equipment for detecting a burst fuel element were proved and all was ready to start to generate heat from the reactor. The remaining work was clearing defects and supplying technical support to the commissioning team and the customers operators.

For this later stage I was made site manager for the Reactor Equipment Team. As well as the technical support I managed the rundown of staff and labour as completion neared. This was a new experience that involved arranging transfers to other sites and redundancies for which I had the help and guidance from the Whetstone personnel manager. The new year 1966 began with the sad departure of the workers and staff but the excitement of raising power in small steps. At each stage, we used the equipment to prove its operation and reliability, during which time we covered twenty-four hours by having engineers on standby at the site and I was likely to have my sleep disturbed by telephone calls. The steam supply and quality were suitable to connect to the turbines and electrical power was raised by stages to 200 MW. Efforts were then transferred to the second reactor when a similar process followed.

Myra was pregnant and we managed to have a fortnight holiday in Cornwall in the early summer with Peter H deputising for me at the site. The holiday was at the Bedruthen Steps Hotel close to the beach. We could have a relaxing time with Ann exploring the beach and Myra relaxing with no need to go sightseeing. The only activity was the building of sandcastles and diverting streams through the sands. A curious couple of old ladies walking past enquired what we were doing, I replied 'playing.' Reluctantly we left for Halesworth, and John was born at home in August with the help of the district nurse and me boiling water but not allowed to see the birth. Hilda came to help in the house and to look after three-year old Ann.

Back to work and the second reactor that had been delayed by problems caused by chemicals used by a sub-contract manufacturer to paint the mechanisms. All those pieces of equipment were remotely withdrawn from the reactor using a servicing machine made for the task, repainted, and replaced. Power of 200 MWE achieved in October. the commissioning of the reactor instrumentation to measure radiation and to check the quality of the circulating carbon dioxide was our responsibility, introducing me to a whole new experience. The sampling equipment and pipework for the second reactor was contaminated by chemicals in the gasses released by the incorrect paint, causing problems with the valves and the electronic equipment for sampling the radioactivity of the reactor gas. This meant that there was a need to clean, replace in places, and retest before reactor commissioning could start.

Work was now focused on supporting the commissioning team through the various stages of the start-up of the reactor, the auxiliary systems that support the power station and the start-up of the turbine generators, to achieve the full power output of the station of 400 MW.

CHAPTER 7 – HEAD OFFICE

As a reward for the trials of having overseen an extended period of long and tense hours over the previous two years I was allowed to visit the international nuclear exhibition and conference, NUCLEX 66, in Basle. I witnessed the lifestyle of the salespeople and met people in all aspects of the nuclear business as well as seeing the plans and developments of the industry. It was clear to me that while the UK had been a forerunner in developing nuclear energy for peaceful purposes, we were now seeing the water reactor technology gaining a significant hold on worldwide electrical generation. This type of reactor, a pressurised water reactor (PWR) was factory built and directly heated water to make steam. The UK and France had been pursuing the gas cooled reactor development with advances on the Magnox reactor but keeping a significant amount of detailed assembly on site. France abandoned the Advanced Gas Reactor for the Pressurised Water Reactor built by the US company Westinghouse. The UK were sticking to the plan to develop from the Magnox to the Advanced Gas Cooled Reactor (AGR).

On return I found more of my time was being spent away from Sizewell only spending time there for meetings and problem solving. Peter H was appointed as my replacement at Sizewell. I was given an office at head office in Whetstone with the title of Chief Commissioning Engineer. While arranging to move house I travelled weekly, leaving Myra to cope with the two children. With a couple of my fellow engineers, I was enrolled in a fortnight-long training course in nuclear engineering, held by the UK Atomic Energy Authority at their Winfrith Heath laboratories. This was to learn the basics of the physics and about future developments of nuclear reactors.

My main task in the Whetstone office was preparing for commissioning the reactor equipment of the Wylfa Nuclear Power Station at Anglesey. This was similar in scope to the Sizewell project and as engineers transferred to Wylfa, we were also providing the input to commissioning documentation that we had to clear with the project team and the customer. Visits to the site were becoming regular for meetings and planning. I became 'peripatetic Pete' interspersing the visits to Wylfa and Sizewell with site visits to the Hinckley Point refuelling project where Gerald S had started to take control of the site, and Winfrith where Winston O was starting to set to work the control system on the development reactor.

It was time to start planning to move to a new house once again and Myra and the two children spent time at my parents while we searched for locations. We settled on a three bedroomed detached house on a new estate at Market Bosworth, moving in early March 1967. The new houses on the estate were being occupied by families like us and Myra very soon made friends and our social life developed. We took the two children on holiday to the Bedruthen Steps Hotel in Cornwall in May. Returning home, I decided that I should give up smoking cigarettes. Sitting cross-legged on the sitting room floor I reflected on earlier attempts at giving up this pleasurable habit. Over the years at this time, I had resolved to give up, only to succumb sometimes after an hour and on one occasion after six months. The routine was much the same, really meaning to give up but then slipping into automatic drive, tapping his pocket, searching for a packet, finding the Woodbine and then the lighter or starting a conversation in the pub and accepting the precious offering without a thought. Pressures mounted: in the project meeting, sitting next to the boss and feeding his inclination to chain smoke when under pressure; the long-distance flights in smoky cabins and the temptation to buy in excess to avoid customs duty; the extended periods of winter colds and rasping cough and lack of interest in other than the next gasper. Yes, addicted to cigarettes. I made a gesture by changing to filter tipped from Capstan full strength but was failing to even moderate consumption now at two packs a day.

I contemplated the medical advice the works doctor had given last week; I might have to give up the permission to work in controlled areas if I continued to damage health and should diet and give up smoking. Myra also encouraged me who, pregnant with the third child, had given up smoking as it made her vomit. I made an unconscious resolution that if I ran out of cigarettes and matches at the same time would give up for good. Taking the private advice from the doctor to try self-control by practicing yoga exercises, I bought a teach-yourself yoga book: hence sitting on the floor and deep breathing after standing on head in the corner and stretching every muscle. The deep breath in, hold, then slowly release, which after a dozen cycles had that same heady feeling after inhaling the first cigarette smoke of the day. Doing this routine for three weeks still had not succeeded in packing-in. After standing up, the first thing was to feel the pocket for the packet, extract a cigarette, light a match, take a deep drag.

This day fixed in his memory, a busy day, no quick drink at the club on the way home, late for dinner, through the yoga routine, standing, feeling pockets for a packet, no cigarettes, no matches. Myra had weeks ago given him her packets and lighter that was out of fuel. The corner shop and the pub closed. In the morning preparing to go to the shop, I found myself to be out of cash. Cunningly Myra was also, and this was before credit cards. The unconscious resolution came to mind, and I have not smoked since that day in 1970.

Life was returning to a civilized norm but on return to work a new challenge presented. The sales office was seeking help on a presentation to Westinghouse on our ability to take on the installation of a PWR in Finland given the name, the Pajama Project. This involved meeting the company's agent in Helsinki and attending meetings with potential collaborators. Meetings with Westinghouse in Geneva and visits to a PWR project under construction in the Swiss Jura mountains at Beznau. The task was to become aware of the detail of this type of reactor and to support the sales team.

Staff in the office increased to include engineers to carryout detailed estimating of the installation and testing involved with the PWR. We heard no more until one Friday afternoon in early 1969 called by the Commercial Director to his office and asked if we kept the details of the Pajama project as he was looking for a ball-park figure for the installation cost of a PWR in South Korea. We had the man-hours and, with help from the foreign office, had background information and the economic scene in the country. A price hedged by qualifications that reflected the economic and political scene was possible, but due to the uncertainties of escalation of the cost of labour and materials in Korea (over twenty percent per annum at the time) it was not a risk the company could take. It was, however, possible to negotiate ways to shift that risk to the Korean electricity company. Westinghouse, the PWR supplier, were keen to pursue the project. After giving an indicative cost, time passed, and I began to believe that we had bitten off more than we could chew when I was invited to a meeting with the commercial and construction directors with Keith W – who had finished his term as site manager at the Wylfa site – to debrief him. He had been asked to lead a team of representatives of Wimpey, the civil contractor, EECo Turbine Co., and BNDC to meet with Westinghouse to put together a strategy to make a bid for the Korean PWR, proposed for the Kori site in South Korea. I came out of the meeting with a clear instruction to explore the possibility of working in what is correctly called The Republic of South Korea.

I joined the team on one of the first flights from the UK to the Far-East via Anchorage to Tokyo; the routines at terminal three were much the same in form as today, but less impersonal and with less obvious security. The Airhostess took my coat and in no time, we settled into our seats and away through the smog into the clear blue sky. Once clear of the land as we edged north, we saw below us small islands of ice on the sea slowly coming together like an unfinished jig-saw puzzle. Brilliant translucent icebergs separated by the black of the sea, then an unbroken mass of white joined by a petrified river that climbed to a glacier in a valley between the snow-capped mountains that slowly disappeared under the snow, filling the valley to the rim leaving the mountain peaks like so many vegetables tops peeping through a snow-covered garden – then just whiteness. The captain announced that we were about to cross the north pole and we were issued with certificates signed by him. Soon mountain peaks reappeared, then ranges, ice flows and Anchorage surrounded by forests.

Refuelling gave us a break at Anchorage, to view the native curiosities and stuffed Arctic animals for sale; then off to Tokyo, a connection to Seoul and the contrast of eastern and western style airport buildings, curious customs officials and then to the bus through streets lined with mud and wattle straw thatched housing and into the city of Seoul. The sharp contrast of fading village dwellings pushed aside, by tower blocks and flyovers under construction. The incessant blasting of horns and the chatter of millions of people. We stayed overnight in a seven-floor hotel, the Tae Yung Gak on the Myung Dong, a market street crammed with ladies carrying loads on their heads and babies on their backs, noodle stalls, bulgogi restaurants, brightly lit discos blaring Korean pop and street sellers of pirated classical long playing vinyl records. We met the customer, The Korea Electric Company (KECO), and had preliminary discussions.

Discussions centred around how the American and British companies would collaborate with Korean companies and labour. The expectation of KECO was that as the basis of the contract was that all materials, equipment and labour were for their account they would pay those costs. Westinghouse and the UK companies would manage and supervise construction and commissioning, arranging for the Korean input by sub-contracting to Korean contractors approved by KECO. The costs would be decided by competitive bidding, reimbursed by progress approved payments.

A significant team of commercial, skilled and technical engineers would be on the site for up to five years. To supply stability, family and bachelor accommodation and recreational facilities would be necessary. Representatives of the three US and UK companies tabled a plan that included housing, offices, school and medical facilities and a timescale for KECO agree. Cars and minibuses would allow local transport to support the needs of a peak crew of two hundred people.

Preliminary planning over, we travelled south by rail through the mountainous countryside into a rural scene. The mountains peeped through the mist and slowly revealed themselves as the white, downy wisps fell away and the sun's sharp rays arrowed in from the horizon in the East. The journey started and our car climbed away from the resort into the mountains. The sea, calm and glassy, without a ripple was left behind. The car rode the stony sandy track, rutted by use, like a small train on rails. Each side of the track was the spongy paddy left behind from the harvested rice. It was winter and the land was a golden hue. The lone tree without a leaf but covered with red fruit stood silently at the edge of the village. What was that fruit? Gam, the persimmon eaten early, extremely bitter leaving the teeth feel to the tongue like smooth sandpaper but in season a fleshy, juicy fruit. The deep red of ripe peppers showing through the fading foliage by the wall of a thatched cottage. In the spring this same road was surrounded by the brilliant green of young rice stretching from mountain to sea to mountain.

As we approached the mountain pass, leaving the deep blue sea behind, we passed high on a craggy ledge above, the Buddhist hermitage. Stopping for just a moment we could hear the shrill chant of a mantra; the hollow tap of a wooden drum and we caught a glimpse of saffron as a novice monk moved about his duties. To the East was Mount Chiri, Chiri-San, from where Kim Il Sung the Korean communist leader was driven back to the north after fierce fighting against UN troops. The peace of the morning calm disappeared as we approached our destination the coastal city of Ulsan. We visited the small fishing village of Kori just south of Ulsan an idyllic scene soon to become the site of the nuclear power station.

The night was spent at the coastal resort hotel in Haeundae at the edge of Busan, one of the few cities that remained with the United Nations at the low time of the 1953 war. After a day to adjust to the time-shift of eight hours, when we took advantage of the yellow sanded beach to unwind and to sample the shellfish and deep-sea molluscs harvested by lady divers, we rose early, eager to move to our location.

Business complete, we visited Gyeonggi to see the four-thousand-year-old tumuli and museum that houses the delicate gold jewels and armour that adorned the bodies of the ancient emperors. We reluctantly left for the airport at Haeundae with the dusk blurred by woodsmoke from the chimneys of the underfloor heating of so many small, thatched cottages. The drive back through the evening mist, the last flowering magnolias in walled gardens. The winding dusty road back to the mountains over the pass and there was the sea with a silvery path, leading eastwards to the full moon hovering over the horizon and back to the journey home. This was my first of journey to the Republic of Korea, commonly known as South Korea, its old name "Chosun land of the morning calm," the name given to the integrated north and south, prior to 1910, unified for more than a thousand years.

Was this the land of war, terrorism, riots, indescribable cruelty, and violence? No, it had been, and still is a battleground for political ideologies, the border between red and blue in the battle for the energies of this busy people. It is now a show of endeavour and has been lost to the world of sport. Has the magic of this journey half a century ago been lost to progress?

Impressed by the whole experience we'd gathered information, made contacts, and got to know our partners in the enterprise. We met representatives constructing plant in the country, representatives of local construction contractors as well as meeting our potential customer's representatives from the Korea Electric Company and our agent.

On return to the UK, my most important task was to confirm to Myra that this contract in Korea was highly likely to happen and that we should decide whether I should go for the EECo site Manager's job. That would mean moving us to the site for up to five years. I cannot remember the answer, but it was something like "Why do you think I've been accepting your absences over the last year?" I had my OK. My first request to John Mowat when I returned to Whetstone was that I wanted the job of being the senior company engineer at the Ko-Ri site and while I could keep all the other jobs for a week or so, I would have to concentrate on fully supporting the negotiating team. He tried to tempt me by offering the job of deputy construction manager, but my mind was made up and he agreed. Myra was pleased and from then on took a keen interest in the arrangements for the camp. We discussed the sale or letting of our house in Bosworth and decided that at the end of our contract we might want to emigrate to Australia, in which case sale would mean we had no anchor to deter that – a risk I had to take. Alan, our third child was born in February 1970 delivered by the district nurse at home.

I continued to work from the construction office and had the support of the services and staff. My time was to continue with the ongoing PWR enquiries from the sales team but debriefing on the joint discussions held during the two week visit to Seoul. Important principles about working with Wimpey, Westinghouse and the customer were discussed and would decide the preparation of a tender in respect of the work in Korea and on site. As it would be a long-term project, at least five years, a stable UK team would need long-term contracts, family accommodation, schooling, medical, security and recreational facilities. As discussed between the companies and KECO, this had been outlined between the three companies to be provided by the customer in this remote area. Communication with the home office, or anywhere else for that matter, was a problem. The time shift with Korea was eight hours ahead, so an early morning call was received in the UK late afternoon. Added to this, the Korean CIA watched all overseas calls, and it was rumoured that it was leaky, making business calls at risk of being available on the market. Methods of work in Korea had to be decided, all local costs were to be met by the customer; working with Korean labour had to be agreed with KECO, detail of the relationships, the working arrangements between the companies on site and the legal status of the separate companies in Korea set up. In principle it was decided that while on site Westinghouse would have an administrative and monitoring presence, the construction would be in the name of English Electric Wimpey, with the lead by Wimpey in the civil phase (about two years) and EECo for the mechanical and electrical installation and test with Westinghouse, taking the lead during commissioning and handover to KECO.

The ability to finance the project was a deciding factor in whether the project could continue. The Development of infrastructure to rebuild The Republic of Korea (RoK) meant that western countries were supplying long term loans to the country at low interest rates by international agreement. Quotas were distributed and at that time the USA were reaching their given amount and could only finance the reactor and main coolant system within the attractive credit, guaranteed interest and repayment conditions. The UK, with little activity in the RoK at that time, had a sufficient allocation to cover the balance of the reactor plant and all the secondary plant. This meant that the EECo could include the detailed design and supply of the balance of nuclear plant, the turbine generator and all the secondary plant and electrics. A project management organisation by EECo, Power Station Projects Division (PSPD), took on the responsibility to coordinate and went ahead to prepare a tender with Wimpey, the Turbine Generator company, the Reactor Equipment Division, the secondary plant coordinated by British Design and Construction supplying the responsibility for the design, supply, and site technical supervision. The arrangement and management of the construction, installation, and test to handover to Westinghouse for commissioning and handover to KECO would be by EEW: a joint company of English Electric and George Wimpey formed to construct the power plant, supported by the technical supervision of the separate companies.

The tender for the engineering, supply, and construction of the 600 MWE Pressurised water Reactor power station at Ko-RI in South Korea, 30 Km north of Busan, was compiled between Westinghouse, EECo and Wimpey, and given to KECO in the Autumn of 1970. A series of meetings were organised in Seoul to answer detailed questions and make explanations, then followed to Christmas. I, with technical help, supported Westinghouse on the site aspects. Specialists from the technical ranks of the EECo, Wimpey and W.S. Atkins, civil consultants, answered questions on equipment and company lawyers on contract terms. The question of the law of the contract was outstanding to the end when neither Korean nor English law could be accepted but was resolved by including a statement in the final document: "That disputes would be resolved under the principal 'ex aequo et bono.'" We returned home in time for Christmas. I still have a picture in my mind of the quizzical look on baby Alan's face when he came in Myra's arms to greet me after seven weeks absence. We heard on return to the office after Christmas that KECO had accepted the tender and were prepared to negotiate a contract with an effective date of first of January 1971.

CHAPTER 8 – THE REPUBLIC OF KOREA

The project planner had drawn a detailed Programme to support the contract that laid out the design, procurement and supply of the civil works, reactor, auxiliary plant, turbine generator, delivery, construction, installation, test, and commissioning. Each of the companies had to provide supporting plans to satisfy their responsibilities and their interfaces with the others. The task was to support this Programme by understanding and negotiating interfaces, primarily with the civil construction for the main task in the first two years to build the containment vessel.

The containment vessel houses the nuclear steam supply system. A 1.5-inch-thick mild steel cylindrical pressure vessel 120 ft. diameter and 239ft. high with a polar crane. It is mounted on a reinforced foundation bearing on rock and surrounded by a 2.5 ft biological shield. UK procurement office had to obtain three proposals for the design, supply, and technical supervision of the on-site construction of the containment vessel as it was part of the civil construction, reimbursable, and paid for by KECO. The contract condition was that the cost of all local content was to be reimbursed. The unknowns and the twenty percent cost escalation of Korean materials and wages at the time required that the customer accepted that risk. A contract engineer was appointed by RED, Mick M., to manage the bidding. To consult with the potential suppliers, an RED mechanical engineer, Mike S, would develop with each supplier the detail of the erection method and interface requirements with the civil construction. To develop the way in which contracts could be set up with potential labour suppliers in Korea a commercial engineer, Bernard B., was needed long term on site to help conduct the local bidding process and support me in continuing to repeat the process for later site installation and test works.

Wimpey assumed residence in Seoul while site infrastructure, sea defences, site levelling site and expatriate camp facilities were completed by KECO. Bernard and I joined them to become acquainted with Korean contractors, visit ongoing power and chemical construction sites to share experiences and to develop with KECO the procedures to engage contractors. Leaving Bernard to continue investigations, I returned to the UK to plan the method, and a detailed support programme with B&W with the two Micks, John Mowat and the construction department. In my earlier work interfaces with Westinghouse, I had visited their site in Switzerland and was impressed with the jacking method of containment build as it did not require a very heavy tower crane, only the lighter ones used for the civil works. We agreed with B&W and a company that hired lift jacks to develop the erection and welding procedures. We obtained bids from two other companies for the supply and supervision who both chose to build the vessel using heavy lift equipment as part of the three-bidding process.

I consulted with PSPD project manager Harry C and his planning staff and with the construction managers of the other EECo constituent companies and was ready to return to Korea with a senior team from the project team PSPD and RED via Pittsburgh to update Westinghouse project management, and to agree our choice of B&W for the containment vessel supply and supervision. After extensive detailed meetings with KECO we obtained agreement to a fixed price for the supply of the containment vessel, the programme and technical supervision. The procedure for paying for the materials and the equipment to be supplied from the UK was agreed. Bernard had found potential Korean contractors to supply the local labour, the one we saw as most competent was a shipbuilder. After discussions

KECO agreed to accept them together with two they nominated as qualified to bid for the contract to supply labour and local materials and equipment to erect and weld the Containment Vessel under our supervision using B&W engineers. Whoever was to win the contract, we agreed with KECO that the price be negotiated with the contractor and would be in stages in line with the construction method; there was training to be conducted for each stage as nuclear standard work was new to the contractors.

The construction procedure was, in outline: once the foundation had been laid and the meter thick shield wall to three meters, the bottom dome plates and supports would-be set-in place, welded, X-rayed, then each vertical stage, the top dome and installation of airlocks. The nuclear standards for welding and the need for a team of twenty-four to work in parallel meant that a welding school and a UK welding supervisor was set up once the local contractor had been selected. To keep availability over the construction period, three hundred welders were trained to select a source of thirty available qualified. On completion, a pressure test to fifty p.s.i. and then cutting an access in the vessel side for completing the reinforced concrete foundation and the civil structures inside the vessel, the installation of a polar crane and the reactor, steam generators and auxiliary equipment. This latter work would be supervised by RED engineers and planned to start in the summer of 1973. Once all the heavy equipment installed inside, the vessel sealed, and an equipment access airlock installed.

UK Staff were being prepared by the designated RED site manager, Greg F, who had been involved in plant installation at Sizewell and Wylfa. Wimpey set up site with a services manager and agreed with KECO to contract the civil foundation works with the construction contractor Hyundai. Bernard took residence at site and consulted with Wimpey commercial engineer Keith and the camp facilities manager to the allocation of housing to cover staff requirements over the forthcoming months.

Before leaving for home, I entertained the KECO site staff to lunch at a Kesang restaurant in Tongrae near Busan. As is usual we were expected to entertain by singing a traditional ballad. I chose to sing the rugby song 'I don't want to join the army.' Shortly after my delivery the shogi screen opened to reveal an Anglican Bishop in his regalia. He said that he recognized English sounds, which were undoubtably inappropriate, and introduced himself. After we explained our mission, he recommended we contact an English priest who lived nearby with his family. I spent an enjoyable evening with Alan and Colleen and made lifetime friends who helped us through the spell in Korea and for Alan to minister to those of the faith in the expatriate community at Ko-Ri. The following day I returned to the UK via Japan to visit the Westinghouse PWR under construction at the Takahama site where John S was the site manager in charge. He was destined to become the Westinghouse site manager at Ko-Ri.

The arrangements I had to make were now partly personal and to inform the UK companies about the necessary preparation for working in Korea over extended periods. The post-war development of South Korea disrupted until the revolution of 1961, following which the government, of President Park Chung He, resolved to pursue industrial development and while there was increasing western involvement, it was not a country that suited the western diet. This project would involve large numbers of western engineers and families over years from the late sixties to the late seventies, and food had to be part of the plan.

Initially the provision of food was not a problem as the pre-contract and early preparations involved investigations, negotiations and meetings with the customer, contractors, and commercial organisations. Hotels and restaurants were able to cater for western tastes and to introduce westernised Korean style foods, Japanese and Chinese foods that westerners could accept. For the more conservative, American food was always on the menus. A large U.S. army was deployed in the country so the occasional treat in the officers' mess was enjoyed.

The supply of western type food was of pivotal importance in the isolated location of the project. The nearest area of westernisation, the city of Busan, was a two-hour car journey from the Ko-Ri site over sandy, bumpy roads and across forded streams. The local villages catered only for Korean taste and the cleanliness of the local vegetables was questionable, irrigated with fluids from the cesspools fed by both animal and human excrement. The only safe vegetable was Kimchi, a cabbage and root crop chopped and preserved then stored in clay urns over winter to ferment buried in the frozen earth. The result was the production of a pickled cabbage high in vitamins, low fat, no cholesterol, but has a bitter taste that most westerners take time to accept. For the construction of the project, an expatriate staff prepared to serve on two-year contracts was essential to keep a high quality of supervision and training for the local contractors. Similarly, to keep reasonable standards of behaviour, a stable family situation was encouraged by having suitable living conditions, recreation, schooling for juniors, a nurse with basic facilities and local provisions. The provision of a regular supply and facilities for dispersal of western food was essential and contractual arrangements had been made to allow the import of provisions on a regular basis. Construction work started on site in the Autumn of 1971 near the fishing village of Ko-Ri with a small team of two civil engineers and families to be joined before Christmas, myself and family, and one other mechanical engineer. The Wimpey Site Manager, John Lee, and the Commercial Engineer, Keith Price, accepted residence and set up the site offices. They staffed the camp and distributed housing.

We had decided to sell the house in Market Bosworth, packed our furniture into store and our luggage into sea trunks and headed for Ko-Ri: a journey the two older children have not forgotten, spending time to adjust to the time difference staying in Tokyo, entertained by our agent Miyamoto, and to Seoul and finally Ko-Ri. Our bungalow was well-prepared for us after shepherding twelve suitcases and three children, although Alan was a bit perplexed. We enjoyed a pleasant and memorable Christmas. Previously, Myra contacted Alan and Colleen and corresponded obtaining useful information to pass on to the UK staff who were about to come to site, about the availability of local facilities, living conditions and shopping. The first group of houses were ready, in the camp with a kitted BQ, school room and recreational area and the perimeter of the camp was secure with a guard post. The shipment of provisions had not cleared customs and the size made it so plain that the 'usual methods' were not effective as a license to import had not been granted. A resourceful civil procurement manager had sourced the shops around Busan and was able to satisfy the immediate needs, but with Christmas coming and the threat of isolation due to snow on the two high passes, all effort concentrated on gathering stock. By special intervention, the customer and the local police chief arranged for the release of the shipment, but clearly this was a one off until the import license was cleared, which took over a year.

My Job now became less direct as specialist engineers and support staff arrived. Mike S and the B&W engineers were to select the Sub- Contractor for building the containment vessel and an NDT contractor for weld inspection. A welding engineer, Joe B, was to set up a welding School. A materials manager, Mac C, was to organise the reception and storage of equipment, buying and accounting staff and local support staff. We employed local staff who were cleared by the Korean CIA, but sometimes this gave difficulties as potential staff had relatives living in North Korea. The pattern had evolved for the allocation of work to the sub-contractors. My role was to see that this was understood by our partner Site Managers as they arrived to prepare for setting up their works.

Settling into our new home, the first task was to engage a local help for the housework and to support Myra by minding the children and allowing her freedom to explore the locality with the civil engineers' wives and, as more families arrived, to ease them into the situation. The second task was to introduce Ann to the camp school headed by Loretto. The third task was to find out about food supplies. Until the import license was cleared, a range of ways were followed to obtain food. The port of Busan proved to have dependable suppliers to the existing international community, including a strong German technical educational unit, an international commissary accessible only by passport that was stocked with mostly American provisions, but in amounts that would be exhausted with the expected peak of over two hundred on the camp. The wives found a way and organised weekly visits where one of the Korean drivers had a contact who knew a Korean wife of a US serviceman who had access to the PX. It became a routine to select the week's provisions from the PX list, leave it with the driver, and the ladies would go for lunch at the Seamans Club to be met later by the driver with a boot full of boxes of provisions. Our ingenious civil procurement manager found ways of keeping the bachelor kitchen provided that included supplies from a Hong Kong trader who had access to an import license and a source of a powerful cheese from a monastery in the nearby mountains.

To resolve accommodation and camp services, a camp manager, a schoolteacher to teach the 5- to 11-year-old children, and a nurse were recruited and joined the site. The import license was granted after a year or so, but selected foods were always difficult to find so visitors and new recruits were always tasked with bringing specific presents and later, when heavy equipment shipped to the site dock, the captain also carried our order of special cheeses and wines as arranged with our head office. That arrangement lasted for about six months until the Korean site superintendent said that we were risking further customs problems if the press got wind of our activities.

Domestic life settled down into the usual routines with the occasional excuse for a party when a visiting official, company boss, the local Anglican missionary, the Ambassador and his entourage, potential buyers for nuclear plants, came to the site. In the winters it was more likely a trip with one of our US engineers who had served in the forces to the Officers Club in Busan. On rare occasions our Korean contractors would take us to a Traditional Korean restaurant, and we had the opportunity to visit other parts of South Korea.

The foundation for the vessel was complete ready for fabrication of the pressure vessel and the start of the outer concrete shield wall was started. Excavation of the adjacent auxiliary building was delayed due to unexpected geological conditions and a revision of the basement rooms layout to avoid sea leakage. Steel plate for the vessel was delivered from the port of Busan over winding country sand roads and the foundation was ready in June 1972. A team of twenty-four welders had been trained. Real mechanical fabrication started and progressed as intended through to the completion of the shell of the vessel to achieve a successful pressure test in July 1973, saw by the Westinghouse and KECO management.

Not without drama, the area was on national alert and a suspect object had been detected in the sea close to Kori. Military planes, searchlights and flares filled the night skies and Korean coastguard troops occupied the site. It was a false sighting as it was a large wooden framed riddle used by the locals for separating gravel from the beach washed to sea by a high tide.

The concrete foundation was completed beneath the vessel, an access was cut into the shell and after the concrete internal structures were ready the polar crane was installed and used to lift in the mechanical and electrical equipment, reactor vessel and steam generators that would be arriving at the site directly by roll-on-off ship.

To this stage my role had been straightforward with two

areas of responsibility: as deputy EEW Representative to support the Wimpey Site Manager in his role as EEW Representative in the interface with Westinghouse and with the KECO Site Manager and the KECO management in Seoul; and responsible for EECo responsibilities for the site organisation to build the C.V. and to directly interface with KECO concerning the forthcoming start of installation of balance of reactor plant, the turbine generators and secondary electrical and mechanical plant. As access to the auxiliary buildings became available and coordination with the civil engineers necessary, representatives from the other branches of EECo arrived as planned, my day-to-day involvement reduced and became more a reporting, coordinating function with regular and ad hoc meetings. The managers of each of the three branches arrived to prepare, primarily to go through the process of selecting by tender the Korean contractor to supply erection and test staff following the process set up for the Containment Vessel, Jim B for Turbine Generators, Bill H for BNDC secondary plant and Gregg F for RED reactor island and balance of reactor plant. The arrangement went well in the first months as they were feeling their way and receiving help from the experience I had gained. As the interfaces on site became real and problems surfaced, particularly with the Westinghouse Quality Manager and KECO engineers, there were situations that needed arbitration.

Resentment by the occasional UK engineer with the KECO technical staff made it necessary for me to take a lead and talk to the person's manager and to reach an understanding with the KECO superintendent, MR Koh. Problems with the Korean staff we employed were rare but occasionally serious: an accountant was found to be approaching a subcontractor for favours. With the help of Mr. Koh, he was arrested and was replaced. Later I asked our senior Korean staff what would happen to him, "He would have the Korean lie detector," showing with a beating gesture, six of the best.

Occasionally I would support the EEW site manager, Wimpey

Site Manager, John Lee, to discussions with Mr. Koh about progress or quality matters. Sometimes I would go to the Seoul Office to meet with Westinghouse Project Director and KECO, Kim Sock Chin their leading manager.

Myra was pregnant with Paul due in February 1974 and our first term was due to complete in November. This was a suitable time for me to prepare to take over the Role of EEW Senior Representative on site due to start in April 1974. PSPD to provide cover for the interface with KECO Head Office appointed a Seoul representative and a commercial engineer to help with administration at site, while I took my leave and familiarization with PSPD in preparation for my return to Kori. For site co-ordination the three EECo site Managers would meet with John Lee.

I contrived to fit in with a tour of the USA via Japan, visiting Tokyo, Los Angeles, Monterey, Yosemite, San Francisco, Toronto, Boston, and home. Although I had travelled on business over the past two years not having to worry about transport and accommodation but was not prepared for the detail of a venture in strange lands. My main concern was driving, as that had been only over dirt roads with little traffic.

The experience was much like appearing from the COVID lockdown.

The visit to Tokyo went well as the company's agent sorted things out and we had well-organised visits to the super-stores, Zen gardens, the pools with Carp, and excellently groomed trees. Ginza with the latest electronic goods, calculators, and toys that entranced the children. The long flight to L.A. punctuated with meals and fitful sleep disturbed by anxiety over driving on busy, fast roads. This was brought to a head when descending to L.A., flying across the freeways that in places were sixteen lanes that seemed busier as the 747 circled lower and lower, and on the final approach was skimming just above the speeding traffic.

Exiting through immigration and customs with a dozen

pieces of luggage and then communicating with the hire car desk attendant was a stressful experience. I thought I understood Americans, having worked with U.S. engineers who had become accustomed to conversing with dumb Englishmen and local speaking workers talking deliberately clear and using gestures and signs. Nevertheless, we got through and a vehicle was arranged, and I cautiously navigated the road network guided by obvious signs to Disneyland. The hotel check-in was easier as the receptionist was an English student on a year out who gave us all the advice needed to visit Disneyland and Knott's Berry Farm, a duplicate of a western town with its bank raids and gun fights.

The kids were enthralled; they still remember fifty-two years later.

Then on to Monterey, now more confident on less busy roads with a 55-mph speed limit. My college friend Ray accommodated us and conducted us around John Steinbeck's material for his book, Cannery Row; we had a meal at a seafood restaurant, and he waved us goodbye. On to Yosemite with its towering cliffs and then round the bay to San Francisco where we spent a couple of days visiting the Golden Gate bridge, travelling the cable cars, Alcatraz Island and visiting the markets before depositing the car and flying to Toronto.

My school and college friend Ron met us and shepherded us round Toronto, eating at McDonalds and then to the CN Tower where the rotating restaurant kept the three-year-old amused jumping on and off as it showed us the extent of the city. The next leg to Boston was a short flight where upon arriving we were met by school friend Carl who, after taking us round the historic city, waved us goodbye on our flight to London. Home to parents and three-month lodgings, birth of our fourth child, debriefing and updating on the next phase of the project and return to the far east.

It had been an exciting journey, yet an exhausting one for

Myra carrying number four but enjoying the experience of the USA. For my daughter who was ten years old at the time it had a lasting effect.

After graduating ten years later she went for further study in Minneapolis and has been in the USA ever since. We visited her in various locations around the States where she has worked as a Doctor of Medicine, and we took the opportunity of revisiting the locations and other friends at a more leisurely pace.

After leaving what was a successful first phase of work at Ko-Ri and seeing the prosperity of the USA on the way home, the arrival in the UK was depressing. The attitudes of the Korean customers, although at times uncomfortable were positive. In contrast, on arrival in the UK we were met with the three-day week caused by electricity shortages due to lack of coal supplies and striking miners. The effect of two years of industrial unrest, conflicts with the miners and the Government introduction of the three-day-week to preserve electrical power, scarce due to the shortage of coal, was clear. To cap it all I was due for a vasectomy operation to limit our family. The latter went well except for uncomfortable movement. However, the effects on industrial production of restricted working hours were becoming clear.

We were to return to the PSPD office in Rugby for updating and meeting partner managers, so we rented a house in Burbage convenient to Rugby and my parent's home. Paul was born in the Nuneaton Hospital and Myra returned to the rented house helped again by her mum, Hilda, to recover and prepare for a return tour at Ko-Ri. While in the PSPD office I met the separate company managers and was introduced to the EECo philosophy: while each company subscribed to joint working, when it came to on-site decisions each manager's chain of command was back to their individual company, except where it was clearly a joint site decision. The role was to preserve that principle and to defend the individual managers against undue Westinghouse and KECO influence. This was to be a tricky call as it was both the US and Korean philosophy that there should be a single mind in charge and unbelievably a vision of an all-powerful driver. This was not my role and one alien to the supply companies. I was approaching another change of direction and saw that my role following this would be more all-encompassing. There was much to improve in the UK approach to project management, and with more than a decade of the experience of this, writ large in the current situation, there was much I could contribute to improvement of our company way. Already it was plain that delayed manufacturing was going to influence deliveries to Ko-Ri. The effect of late changes brought about to the design change of the auxiliary building was giving excuses to late detail design of the nuclear balance of plant and the effect on deliveries of the three-day week. One could see the building delay and sense the preparation of delay claims and extra costs by the UK Companies.

We moved back to Ko-Ri to see meaningful change, the civil and structural work was near completion and with a new Westinghouse Project Director in Seoul, who had a desire to show the customer he could speed up the work. I was now the Senior English Electric Wimpey Representative on site. Although substantial progress was being made, earlier delays were due to unknowns, causing late starts to mechanical works and delayed deliveries as well as avoidable defects in supplied pipework were hardly recoverable without significant extra costs. My role was now, as Senior EEW representative on site, the project representative to Westinghouse Site Manager and KECO Site Superintendent the joint companies' situation and to coordinate a common view. Not always achievable. We had a planner on site, Ron S, who could guide when interfaces were possible delaying causes. Pressure by Westinghouse on the UK companies was beginning to stir opposition to blame for any cause of delay such as late information or the earlier incorrect ground information. This resulted in a series of top-level meetings that I attended, one was in the UK and while there I visited South Wales to see Hilda. I left her after the weekend and returned to Ko-Ri to find a telegram that she had died peacefully the morning after I left. We arranged for Myra and Paul to return for the funeral, and she managed to attend after a car accident on the way to the airport. While in Wales, Myra decided to have the terraced house at Banwell Street improved with a modern kitchen and bathroom.

My role in coordination expected the willing cooperation of the three site managers and required constant vigilance to avoid taking lines of action without full agreement. I had constant feedback to Harry C, the project manager in the UK, in the form of a monthly report backed often by a more informal communication to explain difficulties and ask for his intervention with the UK companies. The administration on site was to control payments to contractors, suppliers, and staff, including the expatriate camp and staff, the school and schoolteachers, the nurse, and recreational facilities. When we did not make up the lateness, KECO would complain to Westinghouse project director who would complain to UK project management and want to see progress. This was exaggerated by the obvious delay that was threatening completion. Nevertheless, we had opportunities to take short holidays and spent time at weekends in the summer sailing in the bay by the power station, picnicking on the beach a mile north, and climbing in the hills behind the station. Myra and I visited Sorak San mountain in the north near the border and stayed in a traditional hotel.

A weekend free of responsibilities, ideal for Myra and me to explore the area. The camp encircled by hills, then a craggy mountain range that spread from the sea in the north and looped round towards the low land in the south. The map was on loan from an American serviceman stationed at the large base at camp Hialeah near Busan who occasionally invited the international community, which included American engineers and the Brits at the construction camp, to the officer's mess to indulge in enormous meals and exotic cocktails that the Brits had only heard of.

The low hills were familiar from weekend expeditions with fellow engineers and families. The map showed paths that lead from the low hills alongside the river to a lake, then to follow the ridge from the northwest to a Buddhist retreat, down a steep incline to the southern low-lands and back to the camp. About an eight-hour walk. Kit was prepared on the Friday evening with provisions for a couple of breaks and an early start made the next morning. The kids were in the safe hands of the maid and mother-in-law, visiting on her way to Australia, extremely happy to have them to herself.

The sun peeped over the horizon to the east, forging a glittering path to the village on the bay and warmed our backs as the path climbed westward. The ground was firm with frost, the grassy banks round the fields showing white in contrast to the green shoots of rice piercing the paddy. The path skirted the fields then threaded upwards. Free of wood smoke from the village the air was clean and sharp, a good pace kept. Leaving the low hills, a steep zig-zagging route followed the fast-flowing river, then diagonally up away from the river and back to a steep crevasse carved by the river flowing in a cascade. A stop by a small pool trapped in a bowl sculped from the rock and overlooking the valley, the low hills, the camp, the constructed power station, and the fishing village with the bay speckled with boats tending nets.

The climb became steep causing frequent pauses for breath. The map was more inspected using the compass as the sun was behind the ridge and the path less obvious. The route following the rock formation occasionally met unaccountable minor obstacles, loose pebbles underfoot on smooth rock and the occasional piece of brushwood in a treeless area. A final steep climb led to the ridge, not where intended but farther north to the side of the lake. The path contoured to the southeast side of the ridge, about a hundred feet below the craggy peaks. The occasional narrow ridge and gusting wind from the east slowed the pace. On approach to a high part of the ridge was another unusual feature, smooth earth that looked raked each side of a small puddle. Time was running out with only just over half of the distance covered. The path was nearing its zenith, and all was downhill from there so time could gained. Near the rise was a concrete pillbox with a khaki cladded figure standing outside. He snapped his heels together saluted and said, "We've been expecting you Mr. and Mrs. Riley, my sergeant saw you two hours ago," pointing to the top of the craggy peak where a soldier was perched on a narrow platform. He then introduced himself as Captain Hong of the Korean Military Police and explained that the path was checked because of the sensitivity of the area and the risk of incursion by communist agents from the north brought ashore in small boats and hiding in the mountains. The significance of the boy-scout-like signs on the path was at once explained. The captain then informed us that further travel was restricted until morning due to risks of the steep and slippery path and darkness, as the sun had disappeared behind the mountain. Instead, the Buddhist respite would supply accommodation and he would take us. An intricately, brightly-painted red, green and yellow structure perched amongst the high crags facing the now darkened sea. A Monk speaking with an American accent conducted us to a small cabin with a patio and table set for dining and facing the distant sea. A bowl of hot water and towels brought by a small acolyte and a meal of kimchi, bulgogi rice and strawberries served and consumed with glasses of Saki in the warm evening. The moon was rising above the horizon, creating a shining path to the coast.

Sleep came easily and deeply on straw paillasses until the sound of a horn, the soft beat of a drum and the shrill chant of a mantra as the dawn broke and the sun rose. Bowls of warm water and towels to bathe and breakfast of hot tea, rice porridge and a crisp crust of bread. No sign of the captain. We gave thanks to the Monk and went off down the steep path, anxious to see how our absence received. A steep climb down the mountain, a brisk walk over the hills now basked in sunlight, following the river and back to the gates of the camp and met by maid and children. My mother-in-law was unperturbed, relaxed even, and said "a nice soldier came to the bungalow early afternoon yesterday, said that you were staying overnight at the Buddhist respite and would be back this morning."

In the latter part of 1975, as the work on site was moving into the testing phase, the concerns about the project lateness and extra costs of the UK work were drawing to a head prior to the commissioning phase that was to be led by Westinghouse. The result was that a summit of the principal actors, Westinghouse, EECo and Wimpey, the co-signatories of the main contract, met to thrash out a solution that could be acceptable to KECO and by the UK companies preparing claims for extra costs. After a series of meetings in the UK, Pittsburgh, and Seoul which I attended, agreement was reached, accepted, and took effect in February 1976 for Westinghouse to take the lead, directing the work and taking responsibility for the payment of all UK staff on site up to the satisfactory handover of the power plant. Knowing the risks of extended claims discussions, a potentially risky extended commissioning period and consequent extended contracts for the UK staff, the EECo companies were happy to withdraw claims. The "Top Brass" travelled to Ko-ri to make sure the message about the settlement was communicated to the companies. I went with the MD of EECo. Turbine Generators to the airport. After explaining that he had spent time managing construction projects overseas having to cope with significant problems he asked me if I would return to Ko-Ri to see the company through the final stage. I explained that it was time for me to move on. My tour of duty was ending, and arrangements were in hand for Harry T, a nuclear commissioning engineer, to take over for EECo from March. I would stay on to the end of my contract in May to provide him with backup and ensure a tidy handover.

CHAPTER 9 – PROJECT MANAGEMENT

On the way home we took a local holiday by the sea at Chung Moo on the south coast and then had an extended journey through Taiwan, Penang and Paris. Arriving home temporarily at my parents, we arranged to transfer our furniture from storage to Banwell Street – Myra's house in Morriston. I expected to go back to Rugby to complete my contract with PSPD where the Commercial Director asked me to visit a gas fired small power plant in Iran at Ahwaz. The site manager needed advice and support in tricky meetings with the customer, as deliveries of the turbine equipment were running late. I agreed, but after debriefing on the Kori project and getting background on the Ahwaz plant, I would take my two months leave and decide my future moves. I needed a period back in the UK to catch up and after reporting back to my paymaster, RED in Whetstone, my main concern was how could I employ my knowledge garnered over the past five years. I needed to decide whether to continue working on the overseas projects as I knew Myra had enjoyed the lifestyle. Spending a week at the Ahwaz site and fully understanding the situation, I made a report and left for the rest of my two-month leave. After five years away and the first renewal of friendships I needed to get back to Earth. Once back at Banwell Street we had the job of getting the newly modified house in order and the garden tidied. The latter was overgrown by Japanese Knotweed and took me much of the holiday, except weekends visiting relatives, friends, and the pleasant South Wales beaches. This was the summer that had no end: not a drop of rain until October.

Reflection on the past five years and rationalizing my

experience with prior impressions, I realised that the idea of an overarching leader of a project that the novels of my youth had impressed on me were purely fiction, except where only one owner existed. I had satisfied my ambition as close as possible and could relax. Myra and I discussed the future and although I could easily transfer to PSPD and continue managing power station projects overseas, we had to consider children's education and the longer term. We decided to stay with RED and use the knowledge I had gathered to help improve their project management. The three older children spent the summer term in a local school that was difficult, as they were expected to study Welsh. Gardening tends to free one's mind to dwell on other things, so I concentrated on figuring out the future once back in the Midlands. Primarily, we had to find a place to live, then I had to sort out courses as it was clear that if I were to enter the wider commercial scene I would need a better understanding of finance, accounting, computing, and law.

Leave over, I travelled weekly from South Wales to Whetstone to discover my new role. First, I had to try and plan a future from now on. The company had no large new projects in the nuclear power field, and I had decided to move away from construction but was looking to the wider field of renewable generation projects. Moving back with the people I had worked with years previously was sobering, but I was met with friendly attitudes and as I had expressed my wish to move into the commercial field of engineering. John Mowat, the construction boss, was extremely ready to have me move on, and the commercial manager was ready to find me a role in future ventures. I had time to settle in and spent my evenings looking for property to buy and on weekends I would travel to South Wales. We settled on a locality in Hinckley close to the schools and at half term we spent a week staying with family in Streetly looking at houses in Hinckley I had shortlisted. We arranged to visit and we liked a five bedroomed 1920s detached house on Leicester Road that had land for future development. We made an offer that was accepted. Formalities complete, we arranged to move at the end of August to allow the children to start school at the beginning of term. We went back to Banwell Street where Myra started the process of selling that house.

The company was scratching around for work for the nuclear division. I was given an opportunity to front for the UK Atomic Energy Authority to help the Government of Peru to bolster their position amongst the South American republics, having shed the mantle of the hard left. The project was to pass over information about a material testing facility and hopefully get the contract to supply the materials and build the reactor. The plan was twofold: to contact our company's agent a banker, one of the few surviving businesspeople, and with the help of a civil engineering surveyor to assess local material, labour supplies and the proposed site. A sales engineer and I travelled to Lima and we contacted the agent who brought us up to date on the local politics, then meeting with the customer's representatives to discuss a plan and agree a date to return with a proposal.

Back at the office I prepared with the design team to make a presentation to government officials and local businesses. I arranged for a civil consultant in ground conditions to go with me. At immigration we were shepherded through customs by a Naval Commander who took the package of tennis balls and bottles of Black Label, and we were driven to a country house hotel. In travelling the area around Lima with our agent, Carlos, the sights of neglect and decay were depressing. Factories and farms that had thrived during the colonial era were now in a rundown condition and deserted due to worker ownership and loss of competent management, either by escaping to capitalist countries or just disappearing. The lack of maintenance of irrigation of fields, overgrown orchards, and orange groves with fruit still on the branches going to seed, was evidence of the loss. Clearly help from the West to rebuild and to support a western friendly and strong country was a political aim, as well as supporting UK industry. Having shown that the plan for the reactor was workable, the proposed site suitable and obtaining a conduit to ensure commercial intelligence, arrangements were made to make a presentation on the potential site. Marquees, catering, and equipment were obtained by Carlos, and a temporary camp was set up in the grey dusty valley making sure the area was clear of human bodies, discovered when doing trial drillings of the area.

The presentation was to the Minister of Industry and Mines, his senior staff, members of the Nuclear Division, local businesspeople, all with their secretaries. The men were high-ranking military and naval officers and took interest in our presentation, posters illustrating the layout of the plant in relation to the geography, engineering drawings and illustrations of the facilities, prepared by our company and the Atomic Authority. After the presentation, there were refreshments and informal discussions, the fleet of staff cars slowly disappeared leaving us with General Vargas the Chief of the Nuclear Division who invited Carlos and myself back to his office for discussions. Our driver and the surveyor left to supervise clearing, so we went with the General in his tank-like Mercedes. Approaching the Ministry, a seven-story concrete edifice in the brutalist style, surrounded by a well defended 20 ft wall topped by barbed wire, the motorcycle escort raced ahead so that we entered through the massive steel gates without slowing, past an officer and guards saluting stiffly. The car entered a garage, and we speedily transferred by lift directly to the seventh floor, greeted by saluting officers and secretaries at their desks. Carlos, who earlier had been entertaining us with stories of former times, became quite subdued. The General's vast office looked out over Lima centre, equipped with tables laden with bottles of Black Label and Pisco, fruit and snacks and easy chairs that allowed free conversation that focused mostly on football and Manchester United. Once again, I was likened to Bobby Charlton – my thinning hair and athletic figure! Time came to take our leave by taxi, when once through the steel gates

Carlos came to life in contrast with his nervousness when inside the Ministry explaining that colleagues had passed through the gates, entered the building, and never came out.

Full of hope, I took a return flight back to work and family. Later we learned that the contract to build was given to the Argentines, the facility closely resembling the UK design. Peru now has close contact with Spanish Nuclear Authorities.

Early days back in Whetstone were engaged in supporting the sales department in probable future projects. I spent time researching the progress of nuclear power throughout the world and noticed particularly that gas cooled reactors were losing ground in popularity to water cooled pressurised, boiling water and heavy water reactors; while the UK were pressing ahead with the fast reactor, there was not a great deal of activity outside the country. I used my free time at home helping with Myra to bring the house up to date, keeping the garden in order and taking an interest in the children's schooling. Ann placed in the senior school (John Clevland), John in the secondary school (Mount Grace), and Alan to the primary school. Paul had two years to go before school. I resolved to improve my knowledge of computing with an Open University course at the Nuneaton Technical College one night a week, bringing me up to date with colleagues. Then with a correspondence course in accounting and finance and later with an evening part-time degree course in Law at Leicester Polytechnic. We bought a trailer tent from sister Jill and spent summers exploring the country. Work soon started to confine my leisure activities as the nuclear reactors starting and approaching operation foresaw potential problems in the backlog of reprocessing irradiated fuel by the Nuclear Fuel Company and the limited on-site storage at the power stations.

Wylfa power station was particularly vulnerable due to potential restrictions on transport from the island of Anglesey, limited to a rail link across the Menai bridge or by sea from Holyhead. The Central Electricity Generating Board (CEGB) decided to build extra storage next to the reactors. The company, now Reactor Equipment Limited, made a bid to build a store that could be cooled by natural convection and could take partially cooled irradiated spent fuel that had been in one of the three dry storage cells. Together with Taylor Woodrow, we were awarded a contract and started to build in April 1977. I was given the role of coordinating the project, reporting to the Managing Director, Everett Long, and leading for the companies to the CEGB. Wylfa has two reactors, this first store was joined to reactor one and soon the CEGB decided to repeat the exercise for the second. The first store was taken over by the CEGB in August 1979 and our company was given a service contract for its operation. The CEGB, expecting similar problems with the AGRs at Heysham and Hartlepool, decided to build buffer stores at each site and asked our company to prepare offers, as we were taking part in the main power station contracts with the nuclear project management company. The company's offers were accepted and were added to my portfolio as were similar enquiries from the Scottish electric company for stores at Hunterston. It seemed that a project with the word 'Dry' in its description was mine. For me, this time was a melee of meetings and problem resolutions in site meetings at Wylfa, Hunterston and Heysham, the head offices of the GEGB in Manchester, BNDC in Knutsford and trips to support the sales team that were preparing with the CEGB and Westinghouse to convince the government to build a Pressurised Water Reactor at Sizewell.

Chapter and verse are difficult: a typical day, dawn breaking, blackbirds singing, bladder aching, sleep escaping, worrying starting with yesterday did not help. It had been one of those days, all too frequent lately. A five o'clock start to get there for ten, giving an hour to debrief before the customer's monthly meeting. Usual excuses but one big one: the prefabricated nuclear grade pipework for the radioactive waste cooling system had been subject to a spot inspection by the customer's inspector who found suspect welds. A complete re- examination by x-ray was demanded. We needed to be prepared for the meeting due in about half an hour.

Usual pleasantries, accounts of progress, then we took the plunge. We explained that we had discovered the defect and were arranging for the supplier to take the necessary steps; our Quality manager was coming to site with the welding specialist tomorrow. After the meeting there were frantic telephone calls, usual excuses, and reasons why, and in any case the site inspector did not know his backside from his elbow. The manager was of little help as he was due on holiday at the weekend, so our last shot was to telephone the MD. One does it sparingly and gets results but must weather the manager's wrath when he must delay the start to his holiday. It worked, minutes after putting down the phone the Quality manager was on the line ears still ringing for having given the pipework a clearance at the supplier's factory.

A quick tour round the site, chats with the section engineers, a review of overall progress, the usual defensive excuses, delayed deliveries, late responses form the design office. Back on the five-hour drive, a stop for a quick ham and eggs at the pub near Telford's railway bridge and home for the News at ten and an account of the day.

Back to the restless morning, I decided to get up, have a quick work out, breakfast, open the Father's Day card, and wake and thank the kids. Myra was already preparing for the day, off to work. I was anxious to get to the day's progress meeting and the endless explanations and significance of yesterday's shock. I think I had convinced the customer we had already found the defects but had evaded explanations and consequences until the experts reported. Plotting in my mind to avoid the manager until I had debriefed to the MD, I attended the progress meeting to plan recovery.

The running of our private life was increasingly left for Myra. Paul started at the primary school and for the first weeks Myra shepherded him, but soon he was self-propelled and Myra free to take a wider interest. She kept contact with old and new friends, joined the GEC badminton club and started to plan her future. The Hinckley College of Further Education gave her access to update her secretarial skills, computers, and data processing as well as a GCE grade A level in English Language – the latter giving her the edge over me. With many different projects instead of a single project to manage meant that my method of work was less focused and becoming more difficult to keep trace of the fine detail of both work and home life. In the case of work, I kept notebooks and diaries but relied on Myra to keep me up to date on real life, which she had no difficulty with.

Having kept the notebooks and diaries I can relate the outside world, but home life becomes more of an impression than clear fact, so reader please excuse me.

Myra took a secretarial role with a small business in Hinckley but kept involved in local social activities, as well as keeping a strong hold on the children's education. My contribution to the latter was to attend parents' evenings and encourage the sporting activities. During this time back near my home we would exchange weekend visits to the family. Mum was happy to visit us as she saw the large house as an achievement for the family and enjoyed helping to reshape the garden. Dad was always there with plumbing repairs to the ancient services of the fifty-year-old property. Sadly, this phase was short-lived as Mum suffered liver cancer and died in 1978.

Focus was narrowed once again when the company gained a turnkey project with the Atomic Energy Authority (AEA) to detail design, supply and build a cementation facility to their concept design at the Dounreay Research Establishment. The project was to safely hold the liquid radioactive wastes that had been accumulating at the site from the fast reactor development. We had to engage a civil design and construction company, obtain a building design to house the remote handling equipment and shielded storage area along with manipulating and lifting equipment. With the approval of the AEA we engaged

Tarmac for the civil works and then progressed from design approval to the start on-site, manufacture and procurement of equipment and installation through the mid-eighties. Routines were internal progress, site, and customer meetings at UKAEA Risley. Additionally, I supplied input to the contract engineers closing the power station dry store projects and the sales engineers developing the Sizewell B PWR input. Except for outstanding financial settlement, the cementation plant was complete and handed over for live commissioning by the AEA.

Our house, Old Sarum, needed maintenance and modernizing and during the late seventies and mid-eighties, while I was able to do minor repair work, my time and do-it yourself skills were extremely limited and resulted in a certain amount of recovery work. I gave into Myra's common sense, and we planned a series of makeovers that I was extremely happy to let her get on with employing craftsmen to do the work. The oil boiler replaced by gas central heating, the kitchen bought up to date, a new utility and toilet and an ensuite added to the fifth bedroom. Once satisfied that we had a modern set-up Myra looked to more challenging work and obtained an administrative appointment with the NHS at the Leicester Royal Infirmary. She edited the nurses' monthly magazine and looked after the artworks that adorned the hospital corridors.

The children moved through the education system with success. Ann gained an exhibition scholarship to the University of Cambridge to study Geography, John took a degree in Electrical and Mechanical Engineering at the University of Swansea, Alan to the University of Manchester to study Geology and Paul to Leicester Tech, later De Montfort University, for Building Technology. Paul converted his building studies to a bachelor's degree at the Leicester Polytechnic. Their proud Mum and Dad attended the various graduation ceremonies, going home to a near empty nest. Myra changed job to become a Discharge Liaison Officer with the Leicester Council at the Glenfield Hospital, taking a course in Counselling and Personal

Development at Vaughn College, University of Leicester.

I continued the part-time Law degree course to obtain a Bachelor of Laws and then to take a year studying to draft a thesis on Nuclear and Radiation Law to gain a Diploma in Philosophy. The head of the law department convinced me to continue with my research with a view to producing a distance learning course to run with the Environmental Law. The promise was that I could join the course as a part-time lecturer with a view to continuing employment after retirement and could also lead to writing a textbook about the law relating to nuclear waste to support the course.

A new company was formed, GEC Power Instrumentation and Control (PiC), to join with the French Company CEGELEC to design and supply the power station control and instrumentation for the Sizewell B Pressurised Water Reactor. Les B (appointed Managing Director) offered me the role of Commercial Manager for the control systems project. With the raft of projects in REL coming to fruition and the prospect of entering general management, I had no trouble in accepting the offer and joining Les along with John H the Engineering Manager and Peter M the Quality Manager in Autumn 1987 in the offices of GEC Controls at Leicester.

CHAPTER 10 – SIZEWELL 'B' PRESSURISED WATER REACTOR

The Pressurised Water Reactor that the CEGB decided to build at Sizewell, SXB, is an advanced and larger version of the one we built ten years earlier in South Korea. What made SXB different from the reactors the UK had built to supply a large part of the electrical generation in this country, is that the PWR has less on-site work and at the time was the preferred design of most countries. A more complex answer follows.

The PWR produces power using enriched uranium: the material used to make the first atom bomb and used in weaker form to make fuel for a power reactor that could be used to directly heat pressurised water to make steam to drive electrical turbine generators. The fuel produced sufficient neutrons not to be concerned about them being lost in the process. The UK had no source of enriched uranium, not having produced sufficient amounts in the weapons programme, and so used natural uranium which was readily available to the UK. The neutrons released from natural uranium are scarce and so the design of a reactor was more complex having to preserve the neutrons for their job to collide with the uranium to release more neutrons and raise heat. The resulting design of the UK reactor was to hold the fuel in cylinders of a magnesium alloy, magnox, that absorbs few neutrons compared to other metals, in a core matrix of graphite to slow the neutrons and increase the probability of collision with uranium atoms. Heat is transferred by circulating carbon dioxide gas to heat water to raise steam, all being contained in a steel pressure vessel. Due to the size of this design, it could only be built on site and construction time was significantly longer than for the PWR that could be factory built and assembled on site. Nevertheless, the nuclear power station at Calder Hall was the first to run in the world and was the basis for the UK programme. The USA were later to have a power plant running with a PWR which soon developed around the world, it being cheaper and quicker to build.

Why did a British company that had been successfully building control systems for power stations join with a French company? The simple answer is Regulations. UK regulations require that the safety-related control systems of nuclear reactors have four separate sets of equipment and connections, the connections running in separate channels for example cables using separate ducts. The US regulations require only three separate equipment and channels. The effect being that the Nuclear Electric would have to adapt the PWR auxiliary systems design and would require more space for control equipment and cabling resulting in more civil works and space. Nuclear Electric had contact with the French EDF who were planning to introduce digital control into their nuclear plant under construction. Digital needs less space for equipment and instead of hardwired cable connections digital, ethernet or optical fibre, taking up very much less space in ducting. CEGELEC an ALCATEL company were producing the digital control and instrumentation for the EDF project, and the company expected that by joining with them GEC Pic could satisfy Nuclear Electric wish to keep the regulations without increasing the amount of civil works.

Nuclear Electric were prepared to use The GEC Pic, CEGELEC combination to reengineer their control and instrumentation specifications to suit the digital systems using the CEGELEC computing elements: Controcad for the control system and Centrolog for instrumentation. This required recruiting control engineers, familiar with digital control and instrumentation and their application on conventional coal and gas power stations. It additionally involved reviewing each of the PWR safety related systems and the power station controls to the equipment specifications involving technical meetings with the Nuclear Electric and Westinghouse system engineers and then with the CEGELEC specialists. There were visits to Paris to discuss problems arising and to Knutsford to report progress and to agree stage payments based on progress. Our work programme developed to include the French and UK design of equipment, procurement and manufacture and site installation to meld with the power station construction programme and the requirements of regulatory review.

Initially our output was limited by the availability of workforce and the flow of specifications to review. As detail of the influence of the regulatory requirements and the computing elements in the digital control system began to appear, the effect on the procurement programme was becoming clear. A significant delay was plain to the extent that it would affect the power station construction programme. A familiar scene. Detail to satisfy the regulations in the security against outside interference was not convincing and was also of concern by the French power companies. Examples of digital control of industrial systems that had no risk of interference were in operation and used for the non-safety-related controls on the power plant.

The risk of delay to the power station was serious and merited top-level involvement of the companies that led to a decision to abandon the full digital control. The safety-related systems were redesigned to run using the trusted, hard wired, systems used on all the existing UK nuclear reactors. An existing industrial digital system could then be used for the non-reactor controls and could still significantly reduce the space needed for equipment and cabling. A supplier for the industrial digital controls was engaged and the specifications that had been drawn up could be easily adapted as could the control desks and panels saving time. Existing designs for operating reactors could be adapted for the hard-wired reactor systems, an area well known to GEC Controls. Not unlike those used in steel mill controls back in the sixties. The engineering staff were reallocated, with redundancies, to other GEC companies. In CEGELEC the loss of orders for the computing equipment had similar effect. Both companies continued to work together deployed on non-nuclear industrial projects, and Pic were employed on renewable energy projects from the early ninety nineties. During this time, I took part in all the negotiations to find a solution that unfortunately resulted in a significantly reduced contract value and the loss of good engineers.

Back to a more leisurely life, my Thesis on Nuclear Law had been completed before working life became complicated and I was accepted for a Master of Philosophy degree. The Law department offered me part-time lecturing in the launch of a distance learning course in Environment Law by compiling modules in nuclear and noise law. Ann graduated and took an appointment at the University of Minneapolis, part-teaching and postgraduate study. She started courses in the prerequisites for a medical degree. She met Don who was studying law and they decided to get married. Myra arranged for the wedding at the church in Earl Shilton and a reception at the Sketchley Grange Hotel. Ann and Don spent their wedding night there after a second reception at our house.

After graduation, John took a year at Cranfield College to study Manufacturing Systems and Alan followed suit to study Environmental Systems. On graduating Alan decided he was too immature to work and took well paid temporary work to buy a world tour with a group of mates through the east to Australia. He earned his return fare by grape picking when he lived with Myra's brother and family in Adelaide. Paul started a course in building at Leicester not wanting to stray from home as he wanted to keep his friendship with Gail, a school friend who lived close to our house. part of her new job, Myra took a course over three years at Vaughan College, University of Leicester.

There must have been periods over that period when we were all at our studies.

Independent of family duties Myra and I took the opportunity to socialise. I joined the Barwell Speakers Club that offered social competition events locally, in the wider area and nationally. GEC Overseas Club had social events. My work meetings in Paris allowed us to take extended weekends. As an academic I joined the International Nuclear Law Association and gave my first talk to the bi-annual meeting held in Bath, on the basic rule of the use of radiation, the principle of 'As Low as Reasonably Practicable.' The Environmental Law by distance learning started with an enthusiastic group of law graduates from all over the country, with term-end meetings at Leicester Polytechnic, soon to be De Montfort University. Our last holiday with family was with Paul and one of his mates at Centre Parks in Sherwood Forest where Myra learned to ride a bicycle but fell off and would not try again. I tried my hand with sailboarding but for over an hour only spent a split-second on the board. We took our first venture in trekking for ten days on a trail along the river Allier in the Auvergne, staying overnight in village hotels. We started to go monthly to concerts at the Birmingham Symphony Hall, to local concerts and to the Concordia theatre.

The work with Pic had eased with the significant reduction in scope caused by the NE decision to limit the digital control systems to non-safety related systems. This reduced the supply of digital equipment and less specialist detail design. Then came instillation of control equipment, the main control room and remote cubicles, and site testing continued. Decisions were now focused on deployment of staff and seeking new opportunities. Both GEC and CEGELEC had interests in renewable sources of power with units focusing on hydro-electric projects. My role was extended to include liaison with the relevant units within the two companies as well as monitoring and reporting progress on the remaining SXB contract. Over the following months, SXB progressed to the cold hydro testing of the reactor and the development of contacts in the hydro-electric business including discussions with potential funding opportunities, consultants, and potential clients. GEC saw the potential for the wider business and introduced oversight of our scope and involvement of power divisions found near Manchester.

The movement of the design engineers and the management to the Trafford Park offices were scheduled. I was asked to move but after consideration we decided it would involve either travelling or moving house. The latter would mean that Myra would have to leave her work at the hospital that she was enjoying, and I would have to leave my part-time academic role. To travel would be a daily grind or living in lodgings. The personnel manager was extremely helpful and found an opportunity at the GEC Controls company that were reorganising and looking for a project manager in the offices at Rugby to lead their work with London Underground. The engineering and commercial work had been conducted with the special rail unit at the Stafford works for years and had been transferred to Rugby, leaving vacant roles required by management, a project management function being one that is traditionally the chief engineer's job. London Underground had decided to extend the Jubilee Line to Stratford in the East End and had been working with the Railway Section of GEC Stafford. A specialist section was formed to conduct the project, The Jubilee Line Extension Team (JLE). The team included people returning from the recently completed Hong Kong metro and were keen to see the work managed with project management experience. I was interviewed by the Commercial Director and the Engineering Manager of the Railway Section at the Rugby office of GEC Controls and accepted. I was then introduced to the project manager of JLE and to the engineering team, as well as the Engineers of the Stafford Railway Section who were moving to Rugby.

November ninety-three was an eventful month. Visit to Stafford, nostalgic as that was where I started my engineering career. Sad because my dad died after a short illness that confined him to Hospital in Lichfield, where I visited him the day before he died to tell him about my new job and to show him my new, works car. When I entered the ward, I was surprised to see him sitting on the bed fully clothed with a packed holdall. I had to persuade him that he could not leave hospital, I was, however, proud to tell him of my academic achievement in being invited to read a paper to the international Nuclear Law Congress in Rio de Janeiro and I was due to take Myra and have a five-day holiday in a hotel on Copa Cabana beach. Sister Pat who lives near Lichfield visited him daily and had warned me that Dad was expecting me to take him to live with us in Hinckley. In fact, he was in his final days and died the next day.

GEC were favoured by London Underground because of the value of an energy saving system they had applied elsewhere. Stafford engineers had developed a computer programme that analysed the movement of traffic on the underground. It could apply to the new proposal so that the power requirement along the line to the train, transmitted by electrified rail, could be fed to the line at the most efficient locations to suit the load pattern through a typical day. Suitable supply and distribution units could then be designed, manufactured, and installed at each underground station. The electrical power, distribution and controls would be manufactured at Stafford. The rail that had a high resistance to wear, was capped with stainless steel manufactured by one English and one German potential supplier. The design and supply of connecting cable, supports and routes were to be subcontracted along with the installation of rail and equipment. Technical, progress of design, manufacture and installation meetings were a regular requirement of JLE. Less formal internal problem solving, and decision making was as needed and life for me became busy travelling daily. The requirements of safety permeated the underground and regular training and qualification sessions of all who might visit the worksites were mandatory. Staff were transferred from Pic to conduct planning and progress of the work. Equipment was delivered on a station-by-station plan and our Site Manager, an experienced railway electrical engineer, took residence on site to supervise our erection engineers and the cabling contractor.

You will have noticed reading this story, a pattern evolves, as work proceeds problems arise and are solved, but occasionally due to circumstances, they attract attention. Customers expect instant resolution not wanting public attention to their project. All the projects I have worked on have been high profile and hence newsworthy and attract attention. Through my story, project work proceeds with problems, but customers expect everything to run to their expectations. Top management becomes involved and must be seen to act. The Jubilee Line was no exception being an important infrastructure to feed the growing industrialisation of East London. Hence threats to its completion were news. The project went ahead to plan during the design and manufacture and was entering the installation phase where progress was visible and interfaces and safety observable. The sub-contractor installing cables was experiencing delay in agreeing cable routes and later in access and in concerns by the JLE safety inspectors leading to our having to report delay and register cost implications. Delay to the completion of the extension of the Jubilee Line led to JLE project manager holding, in his words, intensive care meetings. The outcome of a series of these meetings was for a permanent construction project manager to supply support to our site manager. The Commercial manager was happy to offer one of his project managers, experienced in site management, and I briefed him on the project together with my deputy who oversaw procurement and would be in charge while I was away over the Christmas holiday.

Ninety-five had been an interesting but difficult year but not without its bright spots. John was married to Becca in Beccles near her parents' home where we attended a lavish reception.

Notable was the efficient organisation of provisions for the reception overseen by Becca's dad, Vic. John had a house in Sutton Cheney, to which they returned after their honeymoon. Paul graduated and started a postgraduate course in surveying. Alan met Kaylee when working as a contractor in safety software in London after his world tour, and they decided to get married. The church in Sutton Cheney was convenient for arrangements as John and Becca lived there. Kaylee's parents came and stayed with us at Leicester Road. The wedding was followed by a reception at the Hercules Pub. Fixed in my memory is Alan's attire. Resisting the standard men's suit he wore a modern, pop style, which included knee-high boots into which he tucked his trousers. Myra was not happy with the outfit, the neck ruff, and the trousers in the boots she thought made him look like Jane Austin's Mr. Darcy.

Myra and I were due a holiday in Australia over the Christmas period and attached our remaining annual holiday to make it three weeks away to return to work on the second of January ninety-six. We left for Hong Kong early December ninety-five and met Mary and Peter Ashmore for a guided tour. We knew Peter from Ko-Ri where he was working as a civil consultant and was now working on the new airport and rail system on an island off the coast of Hong Kong.

We flew to Cairns, hired a car and stayed in a beach lodge near Port Douglas. Swam in the sea over the coral of the Great Barrier reef, flew to Sydney and stayed with Kaylee's parents, were entertained and given a thorough guide around the city. Kaylee and Alan were both working in London at the time and had well prepared her parents. We drove to the Snowy Mountains, stayed in a resort and walked the lower slopes and then on to Melbourne where we stayed in a cute little B&B at the wharf side. From there a long drive along the south coast to Adelaide to stay with Myra's brother, Howard, and Annie who went with us to the Flinders range. We visited Myra's cousin, Kim, and family, and had a jolly time over Christmas at the Golf Club. We flew home

MR PETER RILEY

on a direct route from Adelaide.

CHAPTER 11 - RETIREMENT

I arrived back at the Rugby office early on the first working day of the new year to be met by Colin, my deputy, to say we had a meeting in the Commercial Director's office. Sitting sternly round the table were the director, the personnel manager, and the company solicitor. They did not ask if I had a good holiday and went on to explain that following on the reorganisation after meetings with the JLE project director they had given the site project manager role to my newly appointed deputy and the remaining commercial work to Colin my earlier deputy. Since it was primarily support to the site there was no future project work of the nature that would suit me and therefore, they offered me early retirement after my sixtieth birthday and paid leave to that date. In private discussion with the personnel manager, I was offered a lump sum payment as well. I refused the amount and asked to see the Managing director. Returning to my ex-office, I had a sympathetic chat with my ex-staff and removed my personal belongings. While there I had a message to see the Managing director. I made a brief statement of my service to EECo/GEC over the previous forty years and while I understood the logic of my treatment, I was not happy with my exclusion from participation in the decisions made and was certainly not happy with the size of the lump-sum offered. He, being someone who had followed a similar career path to me said he understood, and he would see me in the morning. I walked around the offices to say farewell carrying my belongings and left to spend the day at home.

On my way home I was already planning my future, one of the thoughts being to lose weight and take advantage of walking with the Ramblers. I passed The Island Hotel noticing the swimming pool enclosure and instantly decided to investigate. Impressed by the pool and the gym and the reasonable club membership fees, I went home to plan.

By the time Myra arrived from work, surprised to see me back so early, I had worked out a plan. She did not seem too worried when I explained what had happened, that I was to return in the morning to sort out the formalities and outlined my plan for our future. She wanted to work for another two years and would also like to join the Island Hotel facilities. I returned the following morning to Rugby with that unusual sense of calm as if before a match but with a knowledge of where we were going and prepared for a fight. After apologetic explanations I was presented with a package that enclosed a cheque, twice the amount offered the earlier morning. On the way home I stopped at the Island Hotel to pay a subscription for our club membership and went to the bank to pay in the cheque.

At home thinking about the future, I mused over my working life. First sheer labour, then using technical skills leading to man-management and to project management with a strong commercial bias. Always active, I took part in both team sport and a love for walking, and I planned to keep using my skills and to bring them together. I would expand my work with the Leicester Polytechnic, fully supporting Brian in the new Environmental Institute and continue teaching on the distance learning units. I would also continue along with Myra to support the local walking group, the Hinckley Ramblers.

One Saturday visiting the library I took interest in a small exhibition where a model of a proposed community building was on display and a lady, Judy, was explaining that the community needed a centre for voluntary services in the Centre of the town. Showing an interest, I was asked to help as a volunteer, satisfying another activity. To round off my portfolio I needed something to use my technical knowledge, one aspect of which was already bringing understanding law and nuclear power together in an academic sense. I realised that what I was already engaged on suited that condition by writing for the Institution of Electrical Engineers with the authority of a Fellow and a Lawyer. While I had a good pension and a part-time lecturer's pay, I needed a shield to give me tax protection and I decided to become formally self-employed. I drew up a plan (still pinned to the notice board by the desk) summarising the six areas: Gardening; Health; Writing and Research; Voluntary Work and Law. I fashioned a timetable to give each area periods of time spaced over working days, between four periods each day starting at seven in the morning, then gave myself a title for the visiting card: 'A Project Assurance Advisor.'

The plan was good as a set of ideas and reality guided by the ever-present reminder on the notice board. Gardening, for instance, had a wide scope and included redesigning and constructing the patio, including removing the old wooden garage and replacing it with a prefabricated one. As a volunteer with the CVS, the trustees co-opted me to the committee, and I found myself in meetings including local councillers and representatives of the business action group. The Environmental Institute were taking advantage of government and European grants and I was helping to prepare applications and if successful supporting the presentations. I followed a course with the IEE on consultancy and with the university on advanced word and PowerPoint presentations. Myra joined me at the early gym sessions, leaving to go to work while I lounged a little longer in the pool.

Not all was work. We took advantage of the business trips as opportunity to take short holidays. Ann and Don had moved from Washington to Charlottesville to complete their studies. They graduated in ninety-six and we attended the ceremony together with Don's parents, staying to explore the area of the Blue Mountains before Myra was due back at work. I agreed to help the new Medical and Law Graduates move their furniture and belongings to pre-medical training at Stanford University and for Don a position with the border force near Tucson. The job was to spell the driving of a U-Haul truck and car and to help load and unload. At each stop on the way I was the carrier of the fish in their tank to the hotel room to keep power to the circulatory pump. On the way from Charlottesville, we took Myra to the airport to her first-class flight to London: Don's dad was an airline executive and had arranged to upgrade her ticket. Ann, Don and I headed south following the Appalachians to Nashville, into Texas to Dallas where we stayed with Don's mum and dad. After sightseeing we continued through Texas, Arizona, El Paso to San Diego. The final stretch was to San Francisco and Stanford where Ann had a student flat. While waiting for my booking home we explored the area and arranged to meet Ray S, a college friend who worked in aeronautical research. I flew home tourist class and back to Myra and the future.

The future was not all work. We attended the Birmingham orchestral concerts in the Townhall and that summer to Aldeburgh festival; I attended the speakers club twice a month and Myra went with me to competitions at local, area, district level and to the finals at national. We ended the year with a 'Knees Up' at the village hall with the speakers' club members.

The second year of retirement started as it should – we flew to Stanford to see Ann. Don was in Southern California working with the border force. Ann took us walking in the Pinnacles, an area of the San Andreas fault, with sharp precipitous climbing. It did not bother Myra, but I chickened out when the walk developed to climbing ladders choosing to take lower paths. We stayed with Ann, then took a hire car to see the Boulder Dam and then to Las Vegas. On the way back to San Francisco we visited Knox and Judy Huntsman in Fillmore, Utah, the heart of Morman country. Knox was a colleague working on the Kori project. He had a military background and had access to the officers' club in Busan and would entertain us to a choice of cocktails. Then back to England and my various roles.

Nuclear and radiation law with Environmental Law and my

Engineering background combined to offer opportunities to write for Journals and give talks at professional functions. The Environmental Law Institute was gathering grants to deliver talks at European institutions. The International Nuclear Law Institute bi-annual conference held in Bath was an opportunity to expose my latest slant on the law and nuclear endeavour. This was the basis for talks over the next fifteen years, where accompanied by Myra, I gave presentations at biennial conferences in Rio, Tours, Washington, Budapest, Cape Town, Brussels, Toronto, and Manchester.

Myra decided she ought to share my freedom and retired. I think she had seen enough of old people becoming incapacitated and decided to escape and enjoy the freedom of travel. Ann came over by herself and Kaylee and Alan joined us. We arranged a surprise celebration. Myra, Ann, and I were to spend a couple of days at the Aldeburgh festival while the family set up a garden party for our return. A marquee on the lawn with a pig-roast and a jazz trio, set to blast off on the instant of our return. On our way from Aldeburgh, we met a tremendous rainstorm and I thought that would have upset our plan. The rain eased, the sun came out and as we arrived the jazz band opened with "Hello Dolly" and a reception with forty friends and relatives greeting the retiree.

Myra had picked her retirement exactly right as ninety-seven was a year of travel opportunities. Brian for the environmental Law Institute had secured a grant for a lecture to the Technical University of Budapest on aspects of the law on engineering projects. I was offered accommodation in the university and took Myra. While there we visited the highlights of the city including a realistic enactment of the uprisings, the Chain Bridge, and the art deco of the thermal baths. I returned for preparation of the environmental law summer examinations.

Invited to give a talk to the INLA Congress in Tours, we travelled to France by car ferry with our camping equipment staying overnight at the fishing village of Cancale, famed for its oysters, before travelling on to the congress hotel. The talk on the regulation of radioactive processes was well received by the members and we enjoyed the socialising and visits to historical chateau. From Tours into Germany, staying near Freiburg a university city in the Black Forest. We visited the baths at Baden-Baden a spa town. Although very relaxing, this was a slight shock as bathing was in the nude, and while the treatment was segregated, the bathing was mixed. Heidelberg was our next stop where we walked the Philosophers Way – a steep path overlooking the town. Travelled to Switzerland camped at Interlaken and enjoyed the mountain air. We moved on to Austria walking in the Tyrol mountains and then the Bremmer Pass to Italy. We camped where convenient in frequent camp sites all giving excellent facilities.

Camping in south of Florence, it was convenient to visit the busy town to see the renaissance art, but we did not see da Vinci's masterpieces due to the long queues. Due to shortage of time, we travelled back through France to Calais and the ferry to Dover and home. There would be opportunities to explore France in the coming years.

Having returned, I continued to help promote the pursuit of a voluntary centre with the business group in support. The project name changed to the Millenium Centre to give a finite time scale to the endeavour. As well as the regular speakers club meetings and competitions, I joined the retired businessmen's Probus club that met for lunch and a talk twice a month. I agreed to give a talk to the club when asked. My past activities had not disappeared: GEC commercial manager approached me to give aid in settling claims with the Jubilee Line project sub-contractors. It was well paid, so I did not refuse and attended when requested over about two months.

Myra decided to take a voluntary role with the Citizens Advice Bureau in Hinckley. Her work with Leicester Local Authority qualified her to give advice about care and costs of care. She could arrange her timing to suit circumstances – the office was a ten-minute walk – and it was convenient and interesting. We celebrated Myra's birthday with Ann and Becca in a walk over Old John in Charnwood and then at the Bradgate Arms. Joshua our first grandson was born to Becca the next day. From then our interest diverted in that direction as he grew, and Becca needed relief from caring.

The idea of writing a textbook on nuclear and radiation law had been brewing for two years. Professor Hawke was encouraging me and arranged for us to meet Ashgate the publisher. We met at the Institution of Electrical Engineers, Savoy Place on the bank of the river Thames, had lunch, and I explained the plan to use my M. Phil thesis as a base for a textbook on the law of radioactive practices. After further discussions, a contract was agreed, and another task added to my portfolio with a horizon of three years.

Brian topped the year with a contract to talk to the University of Prague on Environmental Law and in the same week, a talk to a business group in Istanbul arranged by the Financial Times. We took the opportunity to cross the Bosphorus to see the Blue Mosque. On to the Czech Republic, we stayed in student quarters at Charles University near the Charles Bridge and the animated clock in the Town Square. We visited Ann before she finished at Stanford to move to a training position in San Francisco, discovering that she and Don had decided to separate as their jobs were incompatible with a settled life.

Ninety-nine was the year of Shopmobility. With the Town Business Group taking responsibility for progressing the Millennium Centre, the CVS focused its attention on creating a facility to provide disabled people with transport around Hinckley. The principle of Shopmobility well set up: a centrally found office close to a carpark with a stock of electrically motorised mobility scooters. Our job was to promote the idea and arrange with the council to form a management team to set up and cost the system for the Town Council to agree, finance and employ a manager. Supported by an influential disabled man, Peter, the details went ahead rapidly and by the middle of the year the scheme was working from an office next to the covered carpark in the Britannia Centre with six scooters and a manager.

Paul and Gail were married in July with the reception in a marquee on the lawn. They decided to move away from Hinckley as Paul's work centred around Northampton and they eventually settled in Stony Stratford on the route of the Roman Watling Street.

We decided to walk the Offa's Dike, a one-hundred-and-eighty-mile route from the south coast of Wales to the north coast following the remains of a wall that Offa the King of Mercia constructed to keep the Celts out. An early Donald Trump. The route was well defined with accommodation at reasonable walking distance between stops. Using information provided by the Offa association we plotted the trek in two parts to take over two years of holidays. The first in ninety-nine was from Prestatyn to Knighton, about half-way and spaced over nine days. We chose accommodation that was close to the trail and offered transport so that we could drive to each day's start point and reaching our destination I would have a lift to collect the car and overnight bags. Myra confirmed each booking, and the arrangement went smoothly. The walking for the first forty miles was steeply hilly to Llanbedr and Trevor, then less so as we neared the river valley and Knighton. We met people travelling from the south, but only met one other group going the same direction as us. One group of men from a village near Hinckley had come all the way from Chepstow carrying all their overnight requirements. They persuaded us to take their used clothes back – a surprise to their wives when we delivered the smelly parcels.

In the autumn we visited Prague again to follow up the earlier session and took the opportunity to continue to Vienna where we visited the Schonbrunn Palace and listened to the String Orchestra in the Orangery.

The INLA bi-annual congress ninety-nine, Nuclear Inter Jura, was in Washington at the Willard Hotel near the White House. Previously when we visited Ann, who was studying medicine at Georgetown University, we stayed at their apartment so this would be luxury. We decided to make a holiday of the trip and to visit Vermont to see the canopy of the fall. Myra organised our flights and accommodation in Boston and Vermont.

We met Ann, who had travelled from San Francisco, and drove to Portland (staying in a Swiss Chalet) and then for four days in Stowe, a picturesque village where we sampled the trails, enjoyed the changing colours of the Maple forests and the scenery. From there we travelled to Washington, stayed in the Willard Hotel near the White House and listened to the proceedings of the conference over four days and enjoyed the entertainment, including visits to the Supreme Court. The talk on the Precautionary Principle went well. We left from Dulles International Airport and arrived home in time for the birth of our second grandson Sam. Our potential child-minding effort increased.

CHAPTER 12 – AN ACADEMIC VENTURE

The start of the second millennium passed without the upsets that pundits had been forecasting: no mass misfunctioning of the computer-based data systems. We took a two-week trip to Madeira, where the arriving flight was alarming as the airstrip is perched on a cliff. We hired a car and toured the island. The narrow roads clinging to the sides of mountain passes gave little room to pass trucks on the foggy slopes. Impressions mostly of the Levada, narrow canals that carry water to the various villages around the Island. A good opportunity to visit by walking them to the remoter parts, although tricky at times negotiating low tunnels and narrow paths.

The Institution were interested in the developing environmental regulations in their activities and were keen to accept papers and articles from me. The Science and Education Journal published my article on the four principles of the law of environment protection: prevention, precaution, proportionality and the polluters pay. The Engineering Management Journal published my article on the interpretation of the Rio Declaration, The Precautionary Principle, and its Practice.

Ann visited in March, and we visited Iris and John, colleagues in Korea, staying in their farmhouse east of Manchester. Invited to talk to a local branch of INLA in Brussels, I drove and took the opportunity to visit Bruges, seeing the thriving market and the curious bell tower.

In May we walked the second half of the Offa's Dyke trail starting from Knighton, staying in Hay-on-Wye during the annual book festival. We took the opportunity to browse and attend talks. Along the Black Mountains we stayed in a hotel that claimed to have housed the Cavalier escaping from the Roundheads that was a model for Shakespear's Falstaff. We travelled through Monmouth to Chepstow, where we found our lift home.

Shopmobility formally launched in the Britannia Centre by our local Member of Parliament. The local business group were getting involved in regional politics and asked me to go with the local councillors to the Regional Assembly meetings. The enthusiasm of the local businesspeople was encouraged by the hope of government delegating powers to the regions. It happened in the metropolitan cities, but interest tapered out in the East Midlands, due to rivalling large cities. John Prescott's vision faded with only London, Newcastle and Manchester benefiting. We fulfilled our baby-sitting role, keeping an eye on Joshua and Sam to give Becca respite.

Ann, working in the dialysis department of the San Francisco Hospital, had formed a relationship with Rudy, a colleague, and was living in his house in Corte Madera on the north shore of the bay. We took a three-week holiday, stayed with them and met Rudy's mother Leila who was from San Salvadore. The small-town Corte Madera is a short walk from Golden Hind Passage where we stayed, and so was convenient for the American breakfast that we enjoyed as a family routine on Sundays at a small café run by a Korean family. Mount Tan rises sharply at the edge of the town with convenient paths to the summit at over three thousand feet. We visited the redwood forests and climbed Mount Tan. Travelling to southern California we spent time in Yosemite marvelling the redwoods and watching the climbers.

Reading my notes for this period it is noticeable the number of occasions that we attended the private hospital our medical insurance recommended. Suspect making sure we had our money's worth and partially the change of lifestyle to one of less tension; but mostly to do with our internals that occur in the aging body. On return home I had a series of examinations to discover the cause of pains in the gut that continued into the new year, a colonoscopy and the removal of a polyp that was, thankfully, benign. Myra's examinations earlier had revealed the need for the replacement of the lenses on both eyes. Operations were successful and while healing, we took time to visit old friends – Knox and Judy who were visiting London from Filmore.

In the spring we visited the Eden Project, a botanical garden constructed under geodetic domes in a disused China-clay pit near St Austell. Three transparent domes enclosed plants and trees from tropical to temperate climates. Outside were gardens of traditional European nature. Close by were the Lost Gardens of Heligan, named because the workers that tended the gardens were drafted to fight in the trenches of the first world war and did not return. The gardens became overgrown and remained so until they recovered in the nineties.

Less activity on the voluntary front, due to the tightening finance from the council, apart from checking the Shopmobility operation that was much in use. I was busy on the law front preparing material for a paper on environmental law and sustainable development for presentation to the Nuclear Law Congress in Budapest. Invited to take part as a lecturer on the interpretation of nuclear law at the International Law School in Montpelier, I spent a pleasant visit with Myra, delivering a lecture and sightseeing.

Ann, Rudy and Leila stayed with us over Christmas. We introduced them to relatives and took Leila to see the home of pop singer Engelbert Humperdinck who lived near Leicester and of whose fan club she was a member. Heather, a cousin on mother's side, held a family get-together in Rugeley where we renewed contact with relatives. John and Becca took the two young boys to visit Ann and Rudy in San Francisco. Myra and I went to Australia to stay with Alan and Kaylee, travelled with them to the Blue Mountains and to Brisbane where Kaylee's parents had moved after retirement. We broke our journey home to see Mary and Peter in Hong Kong.

Six years into retirement with a good pension and a steady job. Although working voluntarily, I was paid in part by teaching in the Law School at Leicester De Montfort University and supported by expenses for visits by the Environmental Law Institute. Support to the International School of Nuclear Law and the Nuclear Inter Jura bi-annual Congresses was also partially provided. The opportunity to meet colleagues and take Myra was sufficient compensation. Support to Voluntary Action and Shopmobility was entirely voluntary.

This year I agreed with Ashgate Publishers to produce a textbook *Nuclear Waste Law Policy and Pragmatism* with two years to complete it. Professor Hawke agreed to review the work in stages which was of great benefit; but, giving me less freedom to travel. The regional energy strategy led to the formation of an energy task group that I contributed to. We managed to find time for holiday walking with the Ramblers in the hills of Andalucia bordering Spain's southern coast, attending Peter Chard's wedding celebration in the Lake District, we stayed in the Ramblers Hotel to take days walking. I attended the first of the old nuclear construction workers bi-monthly meetings that continue to this day. Baby-sitting extended to school visits and sports events, intensified as Becca's pregnancy was nearing Joe's birth in September.

The year ended with a two-week holiday in Florida staying briefly in Miami Beach, Key West to see the autumn sunset, stayed in the Conch House and visited Hemingway's home. We walked in the Everglades avoiding the mosquitoes and visited Naples. We then flew to San Francisco for Christmas, welcomed Joaquin to the world and then to Ann and Rudy's wedding.

The year began on a sombre note for the Voluntary service as it was clear the council had decided the volunteer hub was no longer on their priority list. The cost of renovating the council building, including removing the asbestos insulation, was incompatible with upgrading the leisure centre for similar reasons and at the same time building a new community building. It was in the air that the council building be demolished, built in a separate location and the space created used to build a more user-friendly leisure centre. The existing leisure centre was demolished – the land offered for the construction of living space.

The book was going ahead well towards the grinding job of editing that kept me desk bound. But not entirely: the Nuclear Congress was due in Cape-Town, and I was invited to talk on the law related to nuclear waste, which was convenient as I was deep in writing on the subject. We went to the congress and enjoyed the Mount Nelson Hotel, the meetings and functions, including a visit to Steenberg vineyard. Following the congress, we toured the Garden Route that runs along the south coast to George. Back to climb the Table Mountain and to the Kruger Park for a three-day safari. Leaving from Johannesburg airport we saw the end of Saddam on the television and the hauling down of his statue.

I gave a talk to the Institute of Chemicals meeting in Oxford staying one night in the student accommodation. Ann, Rudy, and Joaquin visited, and we went with them to Berlin where they were attending a medical conference on kidney diseases. We performed our babysitting role for three days enjoying the sights including the remnants of the wall that the communists built around the city.

It was a bitter-sweet year: the funeral of Alan Messom and colleagues of earlier years, weddings, and reunions. The book was sent to the publisher for review giving me more to do editing. Myra finished her volunteer work with the Citizens Advice Bureau but eager to keep active she volunteered to help on a part-time basis in the booking office of the Concordia theatre in Hinckley.

My accounts of our life tend to miss the routine that

forms the background to what we do. An example being my attendance at the Speakers Club, a regular fortnightly meeting from September to May. I started in the eighties and continue. During that time for various terms, I have served as committee secretary and chair and served the Southeast Midlands area as President. A couple of old students and colleagues' groups on less frequent occasions. With Myra, I attended a regular concert by the City of Birmingham Symphony Orchestra and the Leicester Literary and Philosophical Society. Essential but mundane activities, particularly when our careers were missing. Our walking with the Hinckley Ramblers became a regular Sunday (and for Myra, Tuesday) walk. Sometimes I walked with the Tuesday Group, but I needed time to research and write to meet the 2004 publication of the Textbook.

CHAPTER 13 – SHADES OF BLUE

2004: staying with Paul, Gail, John, and family and then on to San Francisco to Ann and family. A week of tourism and child-minding and then on to Sydney with Alan and Kaylee in Annandale. We flew to Alice Springs for a tour round Uluru, that red feature protruding from the desert earlier called Ayres Rock. We camped overnight and dined under the stars seeing the Milky Way through the clear atmosphere. From Annandale we went to the coast by bus and walked to Manley, enjoying a cool swim at a secluded beach. We visited Kaylee's parents Muriel and Ivan in Brisbane and back to San Francisco then home. While it took longer to arrive in Australia, the shorter distances of each leg were less tiring and, as they say, killed two birds with one stone.

Voluntary activities were limited to participation in the management committee for Shopmobility as Voluntary Action budget was severely limited. This was convenient given that my time taken in editing the book in line with Ashgate's suggestions. Lecturing at the Study Weekends on the PGD/MA distance learning course, preparing, updating course material, and visiting the Nuclear Law School in Montpelier to lecture.

With Paul, Gail and Myra, we walked the West Highland Way in June. An eight-day trek staying at pre-booked lodging and having overnight luggage collected each morning to deliver at the next day's location. We started at Milngavie just north of Glasgow walked to Draymen avoiding the temptation to stop at the Glen Coyne distillery, to Paul's disappointment. Then towards Rowardennan along the edge of Loch Lomond, following a rocky route of boulder strewn landscape. We stayed at Inveraman, then past Kings Field where Robert the Bruce fell in 1306, to Tyndrum following the routes of old drovers and military roads. Journeying across Rannoch Moor, the weather was fortunately pleasant, as it is easy to lose direction when foggy. Overnighting in Kinlochleven, we then passed Glen Coe and the final stretch up the devil's steps to Fort William. We stayed for two nights, decided not to scale Ben Nevis, and while Paul and Gail shopped, Myra and I took the train back to our car, drove back to Fort William collected them and after a celebratory evening journeyed home.

Ann was due to give birth to Seren by caesarean section. We went to look after Joaquin, staying for three weeks investigating the area with Joaquin in a pram and entertained by Leila at her home and at local restaurants. We had not long been home when we went for a rambler's holiday for a week in Alentejo on the border of Portugal with Spain. Walking rocky ridges past forts and fortified villages, staying in local restaurants. The year ended in an unexpected invite to a reunion of the Jubilee Line GEC team in Rugby, a pleasing experience only capped by a New Year's 'Knees-Up' at the Elmesthorpe Village Hall for the start of 2005.

January was spent in San Francisco visiting Ann Rudy Joaquin and Seren, visiting Monterey where we stayed in one of Ann's colleagues' houses. We were back for Seren's christening and home. A short visit to Swansea visiting Ray and Myra's relations Diane and Mike. Diane has Parkinson's disease and was having increasing difficulties walking. Not long, and off again with the Ramblers on a two-week walking tour of the Sorrento Peninsula, visits to Pompeii, Herculaneum, the Island of Ischia, and the Amalfi Coast.

Myra had a hysterectomy and was in hospital for days. Ann, involved in a European Medical conference, paid an overnight visit. She expressed concern and suggested that Myra seemed a little vague, the effect of the anaesthetic, but should visit the GP. Not a good year for health: Jill's daughter Josephine was admitted to hospital for observation, contacted sepsis and died suddenly. Diane's mum Caenwen, Myra's Aunt, died after a lengthy illness. Good news – Finn was born to Gail our sixth grandchild.

We resumed our tourism with visits to Nimes and Carcassonne enroute to Montpelier for the Nuclear Law School. This was followed by a flight to Trieste, driving to Slovenia for the Nuclear Inter Jura at Portoroz. After the congress we toured to Lake Bled and the battlefields of the World Wars on the Italian border. We returned to Trieste via Venice for a walk around to get the essence of the city but no time to join the queues to galleries and museums. The year was completed with brother Richard and Libby on a walking holiday on the Greek Island of Samos.

Adventures continued into 2006, interlaced with medical consultations and child-minding. We visited Ann in San Francisco with excursions to Mendocino, noted for its hippy reputation and redwood forests, and to Yosemite with Ann and the family. Returning from Yosemite it snowed, and chains were necessary. A family joke: Rudy put chains on the rear wheels of his front wheel drive car and ended up in the ditch, fortunately on a quiet road. No harm except embarrassment. Before leaving for home, we went to a Mozart concert at the San Francisco Symphony Hall.

We travelled to Rome and drove south to Abruzzo and to the mountain town of Carunchio where Collen has a house: part of a holiday venture where her daughter Claire has set up a resort, Peaceful Retreats. The town was populated with retired, mostly lady survivors from wartime battles. We received news that Knox arrived, our seventh grandchild, Australian. More childminding? Flying to Vancouver for a Ramblers Holiday we toured the resorts in Vancouver Island, visited the botanical gardens and relaxed after the long flight. Resorts of Banf, Whistler, and Jasper permitted us to for walk and see the wildlife.

A limited family get-together combined with teaching duties at Montpelier, Ann and family and Paul with Gail joined us. We travelled in a hired van to accommodation in Nimes, visiting the area (and notably the asylum) in which Vincent Van Gough spent his final years. Spending a week with John's family and friends at the La Plague ski resort, we walked the snowy trails and enjoyed seeing the children skiing. Then it was home for Christmas with Paul, Gail, baby Finn and Gail's relations.

Interspersed throughout this travel epic of a year were trustee meetings of Voluntary Action leading to dissolution in September. Of the few weeks we were at home we walked with the Hinckley Ramblers on Sundays, usually travelling car-sharing, and joined Myra on Tuesday's local walks with Ramblers when I was not pressed by office duties.

During the times Ann saw us at home she persuaded us to see the doctor. With her spaced visits she had noticed that Myra was behaving in a way that showed she had memory problems. Myra was reluctant, but Ann persisted and on our first visit to see Dr Dale he thought it was slight depression and prescribed medication. As we had medical insurance, he arranged for a private brain scan. The reported outcome was shrinkage of the cortex that was not abnormal for her age. A relief to us but short lived.

Dr Dale had referred Myra to the Memory clinic to see the Psychiatrist who conducted memory tests and made an appointment for an MRI scan at the Glenfield hospital. We had a three-day visit to Rhossili staying at the Worms Head Hotel visiting friends and relations, a vain attempt by me to distract while waiting the scan result. Dr Subramaniam (call me Dr Sub) met us at the Memory clinic, reporting that the shrinkage of the cortex was accompanied by significant loss of the hippocampus and plaque deposits in the frontal lobe: a clear sign of Alzheimer's disease. Initially this diagnosis did not register with me, although Myra took it in her stride. I had had no interest or understanding of Alzheimer's disease until this point. Myra, however, had dealt with old, weakened people leaving hospital, recommending them and their relations of the care available outside hospital. Helping them decide how best to use the social, private, and voluntary services available. A sizable proportion would have dementia due to Alzheimer's. I realised that Myra had more understanding of the symptoms and progress of the disease than the GP. Practiced in the confidential nature during her career, both as a personal assistant and with social services, she would have kept it to herself. I now believe her knowledge and the desire to enjoy retirement influenced her decision to retire in 2000 and to cut short her voluntary work. Best to take advantage of the remaining years without being saddled with the knowledge.

The hectic travel opportunities over the past couple of years are evidence of taking advantage of the 'good' life. There was still much to do. Regular meetings with Dr Sub to check progress and to receive advice were useful to me in planning immediate activities and preparing for the future. A male carer support group he recommended gave me insight to future progress and to plan for the inevitable. The lesson was not to give in and to continue as normal but prepare for change. We managed to keep up involvement in travel to see Ann in Seattle where they moved to work in the Veterans Hospital and on to Australia and New Zealand.

Our walking took us on a trekking holiday in Nepal where we spent nine days walking and camping under canvas in the foothills of the Himalayas, from where we walked through oak woods and rhododendrons climbing to 2,000 meters on an ancient trading route with views of snow-covered mountain peaks. We then went ahead to camp overnight. After a wash with icy water from a nearby stream and a breakfast of rice and fruits prepared by the Sherpas going with us and carrying our overnight luggage, including all the camping equipment

OUR LIFE EDGING UP THE SLOPE

and cooking materials, we move through farmland and terraces of paddy fields, being irrigated and tilled with cows pulling wooden ploughs, to the Pass then following the river to the next camping place. We saw the Himalayan sunset casting shadows on the snow-capped peaks. For the rest of the week, we followed similar routes winding through mountain passes strewn with wild-flowers and medicinal plants and staying under canvas and in hunting lodges, built by Maharajas and commandeered by British Officers during the occupation,

Arriving home, I was beginning to see that Myra was having difficulties in physical activity, particularly noticeable in climbing over styles on public footpaths and having easy conversation with the ladies in the walking group.

But things started to change: the Christmas party where she was missing the crack, as my eldest son said, "Mum see the holes in the wall behind you where the missed arrows of our wit terminated"; walking with the Ramblers she had more than the usual stumbles; forgetting the walking stick after the stop and not responding to the female repartee. A couple of occasions she lost her way: could not find her way out of a Shopping complex in Manchester while her husband was lecturing; finding her way from the restroom at Heathrow and helped by a policeman back to the waiting area.

Over the following decade the ability to converse continued to degrade to buzz-words and phrases, the most memorable being: "Blidiot!" when sitting in the swivel passenger seat and witnessing a supposed error by the driver ahead; or "Shidit" when sitting in the front row of the Chorus at the symphony hall in response to a sudden loud peal of drums. Finally, she lost the total ability to speak. Walking became less adventurous: the inability to remember how to negotiate stiles; rough surfaces became hazardous with progression to smooth surfaces, shorter distances and many pauses through to the inevitable use of a wheelchair.

133

Bodily functions became uncontrollable. Eating was only possible with constant attention, washing and dressing needing total help. Difficulties in swallowing limited the form and frequency of feeding.

Taking on more of the housework and having to help her climb the stairs, negotiating the bathroom and helping to feed, I decided it was time to implement that plan that we had sketched out not long after we moved to Leicester Road – to build on the bottom of the garden a more convenient house. We made sure the oak tree was protected from building by arranging a protection order that included regulations in planning permissions. I talked to son Paul, a busy quantity surveyor and with James, his brother-in-law, an architect. We produced a plan, sent a planning application that, after settling concerns about drainage, was approved. Concerns were that the property would add extra load to an already stressed sewage system that occasionally caused properties lower down the slope in Island Close to be flooded. The water company, Severn Trent, could not accept the extra load of a three-bedroom, three-bathroom house surface water and sewage. After studying how that could be resolved, we diverted all the surface water from seventy-eight to a tank discovered under the patio and to a soak-away in the front lawn. We proved a saving of surface water to the existing drain that, by including soak-aways in the design of the proposed building, the volume of waste to the drainage system would reduce. This was supported by a paper with calculations and test results for the proposed locations of the soak-away locations. Severn Trent accepted our solution and told the council planning office that they could accept connection of the proposed building.

Paul, at the same time as coping with the birth of Mae, drew up a specification that we put out for tender to seven builders. Myra and I helped with specification of the detail of furnishing for bathrooms and kitchen style of tiling, and flooring by visiting builders' merchants. We selected the builder and, after arranging the clearance of trees from the space, started construction in September. Ann joined us in a two-week walking holiday with the Ramblers in Majorca. Welcome news from Australia: Kaylee gave birth to Josie, our ninth grandchild. On return we watched progress daily, taking photos and keeping a diary to completion in July 2009. I arranged a dividing fence with an access gate and visited daily. I kept busy making decisions about the finishes as the house building progressed, kitchen and bathrooms style and tiles. One mistake was to insist on an enclosed shower in the ensuite. We later replaced it with a wet room for convenience.

During the build we cleared out the garage, attic, cupboards and bookcases of surplus materials. Arranging to advertise for sale and negotiating a fair price for Old Sarum, Leicester Road, we came to a moving agreement to suit our transfer. The family and friends gathered, helped us move our furniture and belongings through the gate in the fence and into our new home we called Sarum. The new neighbours moved in a week later.

I spent time arranging pictures and furniture and becoming used to the layout, much more convenient for Myra living at ground floor level, with easy access, guest rooms and study upstairs. We entertained the family and Becca's parents at Christmas dinner. Continued walking but became less adventurous over the following years; I later modified the car to have a swivel passenger seat with wheelchair access, when walking became more difficult for Myra.

The years through to 2015 were much as normal. We continued to visit the gym and swimming pool at the Island Hotel. I kept up with friends through social contact: the speakers club, old employees' associations, entertaining and visiting family. Trips to the USA and Australia, minding the grandchildren in Ravenstone and Old Stratford. The Environmental Law Association afforded opportunities for us to visit European capitals for conferences as did the International Law Association as well as the bi-annual meetings to World capitals.

I joined the Alzheimer's Association Research Network as a volunteer that served me in good stead by giving me a distraction, access to information about the disease and its care. My role was to help other volunteers to make judgements about research projects that were seeking grants. I could do that online with the occasional visit to the HQ in London. It also involved joining a small group of volunteers to watch selected projects. Our roles were to supply a lay view from people qualified by experience: a voluntary job I continue to enjoy.

We followed the routine of registering with the local authority Social Services but decided that if we needed care, we would organise it through private providers, keeping control over when and who we needed. We used the generous hospitality of John and Becca in Ravenstone for Sunday lunch and continued to sit with Joe when necessary. There were visits to see Paul, Gail, Finn and Mae.

I decided that whatever happened Myra would stay at home, and I would look after her when things became more complex with occasional paid carers to allow me to leave the house. A monthly visit to a men's carers group that the psychiatrist, Dr Sub, recommended gave me increasing familiarity with the progress of dementia, as it affects both brain and body. It gave me information and access to sources of help to ensure Myra was able to make the best of her situation. I will not try to give chapter and verse just describe in 'Shades of Blue.'

We associate blue with jazz from the American deep south; a royal blue, however, conveys comfort, calm, and happiness, while the sense of sadness in the blues is more aligned with that grey blue of smoke from a wood fire. Self, that sense that lives within us, may never reveal outside ourselves. Revealed only in subtle ways for example in shades of mood, let us say 'Blueness.' Ever changing but not straying from self.

During early years Myra would describe her life as a royal blue with the occasional excursion into grey blue. Until the children were able to look after themselves the family was her role. After retraining she worked with Social Services, arranging a safe passage for people leaving hospital and needing continuing care, a role that would meet shades of blue from a deep royal blue when a satisfactory outcome achieved to that grey blue of dissatisfaction. On retirement, voluntary work with the Citizens Advice Bureau, giving advice about how to seek care for aging relatives and helping to negotiate the system, manoeuvring the labyrinth of social care. The mood was blue, but it was no surprise to her when she found it becoming more difficult to find her way through the muddy blue of regulation.

She eased her way out of the role by persuading husband that they should visit emigrant relatives in far-off lands. Together with trekking in remote locations that kept the mood bright blue with the occasional drift to a smoky blue as crowded airports and inaccessible facilities on planes made the shades of grey to become increasingly frequent.

She knew what was happening from the experiences of years of having seen it in others, but she managed to keep the mood in a bright blue not wanting those close into the secret. It became increasingly clear by not responding to queries, difficulties in forming sentences and not finding familiar objects. The grey blue descended when a visit to the surgery resulted in a referral to a memory clinic.

Grey blue to grey when relatives and friends became more remote and queues at the supermarket became agitated at the slowness at the checkout. Fear of driving led to the need for personal help and reluctantly he took over. Difficulties in walking and manoeuvring led to modifications to house and bathroom to make them accessible and safe and to the car seats to allow easy access to a wheelchair. Physical difficulties, changes in attention, slight character changes, loss of strength, inability to feed without attention, a special chair, equipment to rise from chair and bed, a hospital bed at home created a drift to grey.

Finally, the loss of the ability to swallow and the loss of weight and interest leading to a slow but painless passing at home one grey blue November dawn.

Although the drift was from a bright blue life slowly through the shades to that blue grey, it was clear that the self was ever there, that longed for personal contact, that was not always there. Contact at the final stages was through expression and reading the expression of others particularly the eyes that say so much if only we took the time to stay.

Activities of a professional nature were curtailed: I resigned lecturing Law of Radiation Protection for the Environmental Law course at De Montfort University, after a colleague in the International Nuclear Law Association took over and retired membership of the Association. We continued to keep walking, the distances reducing to a hundred yards to using a wheelchair. We attended the occasional concert, and I had acceptance from the members of the Speakers Club to take Myra to avoid the risk of leaving her for a couple of hours at home. Kept both of us active until autumn 2016 when Myra stopped eating and a Hospital at Home was set up – a hospital bed and equipment in our bedroom with nursing attendance. Myra slowly faded away and died peacefully in the early morning of 1st November 2016. Ann had managed to join us two days before and Alan arrived that morning, with John and Paul. The funeral service, a civil ceremony we had pre-planned, took place in the Chapel at the Ashby Road Cemetery with family and friends, her body laid to rest in the green section. The procession from chapel to graveside accompanied by Joshua playing the blues on the saxophone. Later a wild cherry tree was planted near the plot as a memorial with a small garden that I keep with bulbs and shrubs.

CHAPTER 14 – REFLECTIONS

Days are fully occupied with tasks from supporting the Alzheimer's Society Research Network as a volunteer, rambling holidays and housekeeping. The Research Network has kept me busy, extended my involvement with the selection of research projects to sitting on grant panels of lay reviewers, peer and lay reviewers, and candidate interviews. The opportunities for joining monitoring teams have increased to include care and bio-medical projects. I extended my rambling holidays to include holidays: Church Stretton, West Yorkshire and with Rambling Holidays to Malvern. I volunteered to help the Leicestershire local branch of Alzheimer's Society to staff the Memory Cafes and with Dementia Action in Hinckley. Princess Alexandra at St James' Palace with the Alzheimer's Society People Award 2017 awarded my moment of glory, for realizing potential.

Christmas was spent in Australia – thanks to Mack for help to the bus station – camping in the forest by the sea near Brisbane with Alan, Kaylee, and the wider family and in the mountains near Lake Crackenback. A week in Seattle with Ann, Rudy, Joaquin and Seren visiting Port Ludlow.

It was a strenuous 2018 including: the first half of the Coast to Coast Walk as far as Kirby Stephen; the Three Peaks in West Yorkshire; the Stonehenge Trek; twenty-six miles with Sam in eight hours, raising over £2,000 between us for the Alzheimer's Society. I capped the year with completing the Coast to Coast to Robin Hood's Bay and Christmas in the Mendip Hills with the Ramblers.

Not a good start to 2019. I developed policeman's foot reconnoitring a walking route near Lichfield and had to cancel my visit to Seattle as it was very painful to walk for about a month. However, then came a successful conference for the Alzheimer's Society Research Network at the Jury's Inn East Midlands. I established a return to fitness with a week in Snowdonia, the Ivanhoe way around Ashby de la Zouch and the Offa's Dyke Trail from Chepstow to Prestatyn – 189 miles over thirteen days.

Each half year every research volunteer has two months to read, mark and comment on six grant applications, giving the researcher at least ten lay reviews and a score. A good cross section of opinion. When combined with the peer review scores, an order of preference allows choice in line with the available funds. The priorities are than evaluated in turn by a lay panel of fourteen, a peer review panel that includes four lay reviewers, and finally the Society Trustees. Include this with monitoring six monthly up to six projects and it is a full-time job, but one I enjoy. The Christmas holiday rambling in Cheltenham was a welcome break.

A January visit to Seattle followed previous years' patterns but was limited by the fear of the COVID-19 virus in the air: the return flight home with the crammed tourist class was threatening. I escaped contamination but was faced with the isolation forced by government regulations to limit contamination by the virus that old people are at risk of serious illness, hospitalization and death.

The next two years of restrictive regulations I will compress into few sentences.

I continued to walk twice each week, mostly alone, and covered all the reasonable distanced walks without needing transport. I convinced myself that it would not be harmful to travel by car and went ahead to walk the Leicester Round, about one hundred miles, in 10-mile loops. As the COVID rules eased I included my gym friends, Mack, Annette, Mylan, and Dave.

Walking alone my train of thought roamed back over the past

eighty-six years. Walking at the edge of the wood, the early sunlight filtered through the lightly leaved branches caused me to adjust the peak of my flat cap to avoid the hypnotizing effect of the flickering light. A train of thought started that took me back to bath-nights long ago. On Friday nights we had to scrub-up and while families had to share the galvanized tub in their kitchens filled from the tap and warmed by hot water from the kettle on the gas stove, we had a proper bathroom. Dad was a plumber and had installed a bath fed by water heated by the boiler behind the fire in the living room. Bath night was preceded by lighting the fire with newspaper sticks and scarce lumps of coal, partly garnered from the local railway line and from the monthly ration. It was the memory of the flickering firelight on the yellowing wallpaper that brought these thoughts on as I ambled through the wood.

One memory led to another. We were back from a holiday by the sea at Ramsgate, popular for its funfair. The last time to be away from home for at least six years. The war was immanent and already blackout curtains installed over windows and doors to prevent even that weak light from the gas lamps seen from enemy planes. The memory of that "Pop" as the gas exploded when the match ignited the underside of the globe temporarily interrupted the reverie. Thoughts wandered to starting school as I climbed over the rickety stile at the edge of the wood. I pictured that first day at school as if it were yesterday with the flickering firelight from the roaring hearth behind Ms. Arthur's desk.

As the path stretched across the grassy hill my train of thoughts flipped to the time of release from that nightly fear of air raids. Dad decided that electricity was the future and installed lighting and power to keep up with the neighbours. Electric light was an improvement on the gas and no lingering smells, even though it occasionally failed.

Musing on the explanation for power failure: the overloaded distribution system would cause the turbines to slow and for the generated frequency to fall and the lights to flicker, dim and then disconnect. In striving to keep the system frequency within limits each turbine governor increases the super-heated steam flow, from the boilers heated by coal, to try to bring the turbine back to speed. If the speed does not recover and the frequency return within limits a sustained high torque on the turbine shaft would result, lead to its distortion and severe damage. Imagine a hundred megawatts of spinning energy sprayed through the turbine hall. Potentially that could happen to the turbine generators on the system, so by system design prevented when, having failed to restore speed, the distribution system would disconnect the load and free the load on the turbine generators to restore the frequency. I had seen the results of a turbine disintegration: it was not a pretty sight.

As I stopped at the top of the hill to have a breather and to survey the surrounding countryside, I remembered that Dad had said that electrical engineering was the future, so my future was sealed and after technical and practical training, I helped to set up a strong and reliable power system by taking part in the commissioning and supporting a fleet of nuclear power stations. The reserve power meant that power is always available, and the system frequency kept within limits. The last nuclear power station, Sizewell 'B,' was commissioned thirty years ago.

My thoughts returned to the present day: cheap gas from the North Sea, wind turbines and solar farms require less capital, less planning and shorter construction time with power companies relying on existing nuclear as back up. The shorter time construction of gas fired power stations will withstand the inevitable absence of wind and sunshine so avoiding supply disruption. When building gas-fired power stations is no longer acceptable and there is no need to have a constant frequency of alternating electricity today's idealism may survive the abandonment of nuclear power. In that unlikely event in the meantime, the government is encouraging the building of two large nuclear power stations. For future development there is also a solution to the large capital cost and short construction for the following years by supplying factory-assembled, small, nuclear-powered electrical generators, ranging from a low power output. So, Dad was right – Electricity is the future.

No longer involved but I can guess. I am feeling hungry and getting close to breakfast time. I had better get back.

The Research Network continued with meetings and presentations from researchers on Zoom or Microsoft Teams. Throughout the various lockdowns I have been able to stay connected with family and friends. Family suffered with the virus: Paul after a post-lockdown rugby club reunion, Sam, and Josh after a function in London. More concerning: Gail had treatment for a colon cancer that was successful; Becca had an attack of rheumatic fever that still lingers, and Alan is having treatment for a liver cancer. Facetime is a boon as it allows visual worldwide contact and WhatsApp offers chat in groups. I manage to send photos to my Facebook Friends with a little explanation of my walking trips.

During an easing of the lockdown regulations, I spent Christmas 2021 at Church Stretton on a walking holiday and now see my story as near the top of the slope. I am fit and intend to keep so. I walk with the Hinckley Ramblers and take trekking holidays. My role with the Alzheimer's Society continues with regular advisory meetings and I attend the Singing Café as a volunteer at the pathways centre. Myra enjoyed going and the support volunteers gave to carers and people with dementia of major help that I hope I can help support. Unfortunately, my earlier role as a local Alzheimer's Volunteer stopped as the Society lost the contract with the Leicestershire council to AgeUK and then COVID 19 restrictions prohibited any alternative. There came no new initiative by the Society in Leicestershire.

I find the current situation in June 2022 worrying: the COVID virus is still with us, although all restrictions have been lifted and care is left to the individual; the BREXIT arrangements are threatening due to incomplete agreement with the EU; after effects of both the above together with the invasion of Ukraine and continued fighting by the Russians has caused worldwide financial effects and continued threats to food and commodity supplies; and the possibility of more general armed conflict. It seems to me that the threats I have related in earlier chapters of our life are coming together at the same time: war, scarcity, and a plain regression in in the fairness of education and opportunities started after the second world war. Do I leave it here? It could be a happy conclusion or not much different than when I entered the world in 1936! But nothing should prevent us doing the things that keep us going.

Once the lockdown eased, restrictions on meetings indoors were being relaxed, with Clubs and Societies beginning to plan for regular get-togethers, including contests and annual competitions. The Barwell Speakers Club membership had depleted over the two years of on and off lockdowns. Continuity using on-line systems had kept a small group of members trying to behave near normal. Older long-term members lacked the facility to join in, others had been affected by the disease and some had died. Two years of isolation had changed priorities. New and improved disciplines, different attractions and disinterest in clubbable activities, had affected membership.

Although the ease of not having to leave home on chilly winter nights was a deterrent to evening meetings and the saving of travel time and expense was hard to give up, the flat screen of the laptop was no substitute for transmitting the three-dimensional aspects of a rousing speech. Eye contact, use of gestures and objects to illustrate a talk are far superior to the flat screen images of on-line systems.

The management of the Association of Speakers Clubs to which the club belonged was interested in return to the system that yielded champions, from clubs to compete with other clubs in the area, district and national levels. The Association had encouraged clubs to use on-line contact and given advice, but to supply a control needed for serious competition online was a task they had not tackled. Decisions were made to institute District and National live competitions. Individual clubs and area managements were to make their own arrangements to select champions to compete at district level either by live meetings or on screen.

The club decided to start face to face meetings and had rebuilt membership to seven that were prepared to meet in public. The local community hall was happy to have the business. On the night of the club competition, two members of an adjacent club were to be invited as Judges to select the Speech Evaluator to stand for the club in the Area Evaluation Contest. As there were few volunteers I reluctantly offered to compete. I had been an officer of the club for over twenty-five years at all posts, but never won a competition and was not welcoming success.

On the evening of the competition, a speaker invited from another club stood at the lectern and delivered his timed speech. The three evaluators after listening intently were escorted to a side room to compose their four-minute constructive criticism of the speech. Ten minutes to prepare notes, the scripts were held by a monitor until one at a time the contestants were guided back to the speech room, given their notes and delivered their evaluations. The judges sitting strategically around the room listened, made their notes, and when the three evaluations were finished left for a separate room to deliberate. After a tea-break the chief judge delivered his complements for the evening to the meeting and announced the winner, the Club Chairman. To my relief I was runner up.

The Hinckley Ramblers started group walks, the pub break during the Thursday walk I led jolted memories of over sixty years ago. The Green Man was a popular pub for those friends who had access to transport, usually a parent's car, and did not mind their favourite son taking us adventurous teenagers on rides through the local countryside. Pete's dad was an electrical wholesaler who was careless about use of his second car, a roomy Rover 12, that could accommodate the whole of the gang. The excuse was to explore the countryside on summer Friday evenings, but the real aim was to include a pub-stop where there would be similar groups recounting the week's escapades at work, college, and school. The proprietor was happy to let closing time slip and often supported by the local copper, if drinking after closing time was behind locked doors. In those days there were no specific laws about drinking and driving but the copper always found the driver and made sure he recommended leaving before consuming too much, so generally the trip home was uneventful, though sometimes a little unsteady.

Memories of those days and friends long forgotten flowed through my mind as we completed the Thursday walk and put the seed in my mind, as we finished early, to take a trip along those routes of the lanes of Staffordshire and visit some of the other establishments. The Horse and Jockey just outside Lichfield used to offer us similar hospitality and the proprietor Alf with his wife Peggy, once a greengrocer in our village, were always very understanding. Our trips through the local countryside used to be following a net of lanes crossing one or two main roads but now, I had to negotiate a network of fast road connections that led me through car parks and shopping precincts. The signposting was concerned more with directions to supermarkets, sports facilities, and the traffic speeding to the trunk-roads. The first shock when arriving at the Horse and Jockey was, no matter how I searched, there was no sign of that smoke laden gnarled wooden bar and snug but a posh restaurant. No steps but ramps and handrails with all the advice to avoid accident liability. The memory of a packed bar with lads and lassies shoulder to shoulder posing and relating tall stories disappeared in a flash.

From here to a lane past the Shoulder of Mutton, now boarded up, where another memory, of my getting ratty with the boasting son of a builder, lost forever. Then to Shenstone after negotiating traffic islands transmitting speeding traffic interchanging between trunk-roads and the toll-road, the lanes completely obliterated. The Fox and Hounds on first view had not changed, the steep route from the car park down a flight of stone steps was still as hazardous as ever, particularly on the way up in the dark early hours after a skin full. Inside, the bar was still there and with a couple of old timers who looked as if they had not moved for sixty years. The space that had occupied the throng of teenage drinkers now reduced to a strip by the bar the rest of the space occupied by neat, polished tables set for the evening meals.

Being so close I could not resist diverting to the Hardwick Arms, my dad's boozer, where a rush of memories came flooding to mind. The wooden display case above the bar still held the trophies for crib and domino competitions. The high stool in the corner was still there, but strangely empty, where once it occupied constable Cope in his thinly disguised policeman's trousers and boots, behind a grey raincoat. If only I had the talent of Dylan Thomas, there were other stories here: returning relatives from the war were not shy to relate their tales that we would never hear at home. Uncle Ted who saw the destruction of the Ruhr and the poverty of the homeless population evoking scenes not unlike those we hear from Syria. Reg, a marine commando sworn to secrecy, but who could not help hinting at situations that conjured in our minds' scenes of clandestine operations. My dad was unusually quiet, I wondered why!

I left for home feeling sad but having exorcised memories.

My diary from mid-March 2020 shows a daily crossing-out of entries giving times and locations of meetings, events, travel arrangements, visits, and holidays. Slowly over the progress of COVID-19 the first expectation, that once the lockdown arrangements eased normal service would resume and so would these activities, has become a fiction. The experience of coping in this extraordinary situation has altered that expectation.

What will be different? Let us take holidays: in recent years I have spaced my holidays around the year walking on trails, the Offa's Dyke, coast to coast being examples and this year I was due to have a week walking the hills of the Lake District in March just as the lockdown started. In July I arranged a family get-together in Dovedale for my four kids and their families, twenty-two people. Both were cancelled and so in their place I replaced them with a trek along the Nidderdale trail in August and a solo Christmas in the Cotswold's. I managed a visit to Seattle to see Ann and family just before the lockdown, but I hesitate to travel overseas for at least a year or two. Maybe I will rearrange a get-together in a couple of years.

Meetings with the Alzheimer's staff are conducted at head office but through the lockdown have been by remote means using virtual meetings. For the Society likely that saving on room hire and travel expenses will mean an increase in remote working. Once grants are awarded for the research – which range from PhD studentships to fellowships to integrated projects in the field of care, public services, and bio-medical investigations – three lay monitors are given to each project and arrange to meet with the researcher at six-to-twelve-month intervals. Over the last three months the travel to locations over the UK replaced with virtual meetings. This has proved that apart from familiarity with the facilities and equipment such meetings are just as effective as face-to-face meetings. In addition, it has given the researcher the experience of compiling video presentations. The time of the Conference may well be past as already research presented using video means; I can see the day when the YouTube Conference becomes the norm.

The lockdown showed the vulnerability of people disabled both physically and mentally who live alone and in care. The dependency on low paid and poorly trained personnel, highlighted by the tragic death rate in care homes and the problems of isolation of people living alone. The promise of an integrated health and care system vaunted over two years ago has not happened and the load and discontinuity caused on both services has highlighted the problems of its absence. Hence the justified praise of health service workers not reflected in praise for the care worker. We are inclined to blame the Government but in fact the problem lies with the public: we would like to see equal ability being employed in health and care but that is only possible by giving equal training and rewards, but we do not want to pay the cost.

A full-time family carer at home can become isolated: friends tend to avoid them, and the carer becomes focused on the case to the exclusion of other interests. The person with a diagnosis of a cause of dementia becomes isolated as people avoid the difficulties of communication. In a society where access is not a problem there are individuals and organisations that make up for this deficiency. In our current situation where access is restricted, that latter facility has disappeared. People affected by dementia are confined to home by the rules to avoid contact and infection by the COVID-19 virus, with no clear concern about the potential damage caused by the consequent isolation.

Since early in the lockdown the Alzheimer's Society has supplied a source of remote contact termed Companion Calls by involving volunteers who contact by telephone people affected by dementia that have requested contact. I applied to join as a volunteer in April shortly after the system release. On finding my way through the joining detail and the Society's training system accepted and given a set of guidelines focused on confidentiality and given hints about conversational approaches. I was given a small group of people to contact on a regular basis named only by their first names.

The first calls were challenging work as I am not a natural conversationalist, however, my experience as the prime carer for Myra had given me two areas of insight: I could imagine the situation of the people I was contacting, and I had the patience to listen. Over a few calls I built up a mental picture of the person: one with early onset dementia had difficulty finding words that with a little help we could tease out; another whose partner is locked into a care home, and who has a wealth of past experiences that come bubbling out with little encouragement from me; another's partner died last year and has a diagnosis of Alzheimer's Disease, but recognised me as soon as lifting the phone, opening the conversation and holding it for the rest of the session, and an ex-serviceman who has stories of his time in the army from which I get a realistic tale each time I call. I can picture these isolated characters from my time both as a helper at memory cafes and latterly as a group support volunteer, until suspended in March due to incompatible restrictions.

I now look forward to the pre-arranged times to call and spend about half an hour with each companion. I take care not to offer advice and keep the conversation away from politics. I make a report on a simple format on screen easily completed.

A first venture in the real world to a live concert at the Symphony Hall, braving the threatened virus still lingering in crowds.

The journey started with a walk in the drizzle to the railway station to wait for a delayed train and the slow journey to New Street. The dawning anxiety was lifted on walking through the nearly completed Paradise with its glittering buildings blending with the traditional Town Hall and Art Gallery. Once stood that brutalist Central Library Prince Charles described as looking like "a place where books are incinerated, not kept." ('Birmingham Central Library timeline - BBC News'). To the recently improved Symphony Hall passing the preparations for Christmas jollity, the big wheel and skating plaza.

The concert, An American Road Trip, conducted by Jaumie Santonja Espinos, commenced with Villa-Lobos's Fantasia for Saxophone played by Jess Gillam, transporting me to Rio. A working holiday talking to the nuclear brotherhood and enjoying the corporate entertainment with Myra. Strolling before dinner along the Copacabana and Ipanema beaches, climbing early morning to Christ the Redeemer statue atop

Mount Corcovado.

The music moved on to Cuba with Aron Copeland's Danzon Cubano experienced from memories gathered visiting Florida Keys, seeing the vivid sunsets visiting Hemmingway's home with its cemetery for his cats. Milhaud's Scaramouche took me back to Rio with Tangos and Sambas and a sense of enjoyment.

Moving north to Virginia and Pennsylvania with Aron Copeland's Appalachian Spring. Memories of hikes in the Blue Ridge Mountains, visits to the small pioneer villages and their white wooden churches. A trip to see Einstein's chemist shop, stirring the shopkeeper sleeping on the counter in front of the till. The beat of the square dance and tunes of the Shaker sect.

Samuel Barber's symphony moved us to the east coast with an Atlantic Gale and the Age of Anxiety. The endless traffic on Washington's roads to the busy museums and Capitol. To New York the cacophony of office workers from The Grand Central Station to the skyscrapers, with slender brunettes carrying their high heeled shoes and wearing trainers to battle the pavement.

Concert over, walking back in the darkened city to the station but moving on in memory to a holiday in New England in the Fall. Portland in a Swiss Chalet and four days in Stowe, a picturesque village where we sampled the trails, enjoyed the changing colours of the Maple forests and the scenery.

A kind neighbour spied me walking back from Hinckley station in the dark and gave me a lift home.

It is surprising how close we get to someone who is famous. I mean, famous, in a genuine way not a criminal, or though I sometimes I have my suspicions. No, I mean someone like the Prime Minister or a member of the Royal Family. It happens because we contact thousands of people during our lifetime and will have been in close touch with someone famous; for example, they may have shaken hands with their MP or received an award. Let me give examples from my own experience. After completing an engineering degree, I was invited along with my parents, who having supported me for three years, to a degree ceremony at the Albert Hall. After heavy speeches by Professors and Captains of Industry and the Queen Mother each graduate invited to join a long queue to receive their degree and a gloved handshake from the Queen Mother. So only a silk glove away.

The next occasion was in West Bengal at the time when Pundit Nehru was visiting Durgapur steel works, where the British were building a greenfield project at the same time the Russians and Germans were doing similarly in Bhopal and Rourkela. Nehru climbed onto the steel frame of the open rolling mill-housing so that he could address the vast crowd as well as the expatriates at the front. He did not touch hands but greeted us with a Namaste sign and he was near enough to leave a distinct image of him in my memory, lodged on the steel frame, his dhoti wrapped round his knees, traditional white cap and shrilly shouting to the crowd.

Also, at Durgapur in less populated circumstances we were visited by The Queen and Prince Phillip and invited to a reception at the club the following evening:

In South Korea we were building, with a civil engineering compatriot and Korean contractors, a pressurised water nuclear power station. Visited by Lord Nelson of Stafford, our Managing Director, not like his tough old dad, he was a good boss nicknamed Half-Nelson. After the site visit, Myra and I, together with the company senior staff, entertained him and his wife to an evening meal in our small bungalow. His wife even went to see our children asleep in bed.

My final encounter was not a near miss! I had been caring for Myra for ten Years and through the latter part I joined Alzheimer's Research Network as a volunteer. This lay help provides the Alzheimer's Society with ability and experience in care, helping to review care research grant applications, a task done at home and supplied a distraction for me in quiet times. It also gave me a better understanding of the progress of the disease than I could get anywhere else. The year after Myra's death awarded a Peoples Award for 'Realizing Potential' presented at St James' Palace by Princess Alexandra who took me by the hand.

We can expect less travel, higher taxes, higher costs for holidays, more leisure time, for those working for a living less secure employment and lower wages, and the return of escalation to levels seen in the seventies. I note I am repeating myself; it is time to call an end to this reverie.

Printed in Great Britain
by Amazon